LEROY COLLINS LEON COUNTY PUBLIC LIBRARY

3 1260 01199 3014

W9-AHL-139

1-04

DATE DUE

SIMON & SCHUSTER

NEW YORK   LONDON   TORONTO   SYDNEY   SINGAPORE

NO
VISIBLE
HORIZON

Surviving
the World's Most
Dangerous Sport

JOSHUA COOPER RAMO

SIMON & SCHUSTER
Rockefeller Center
1230 Avenue of the Americas, New York, NY 10020

Copyright © 2003 by Joshua Cooper Ramo
All rights reserved, including the right of reproduction
in whole or in part in any form.

SIMON & SCHUSTER and colophon are registered
trademarks of Simon & Schuster, Inc.
For information regarding special discounts for bulk purchases,
please contact Simon & Schuster Special Sales at
1-800-456-6798 or business@simonandschuster.com

Designed by Kevin Hanek

Manufactured in the United States of America

10   9   8   7   6   5   4   3   2   1

Library of Congress Cataloging-in-Publication Data
Ramo, Joshua Cooper.
No visible horizon : surviving the world's most dangerous sport /
Joshua Cooper Ramo.
p.   cm.
1. Stunt flying. I. Title.
TL711.S8R36 2003
797.5´4—dc21   2003041543
ISBN 0-7432-2950-9

The author gratefully acknowledges permission from the following
source to reprint material in its control:
Charles E. Tuttle Co., Inc. of Boston, Massachusetts and Tokyo, Japan
for four haiku from Japanese Death Poems, edited by Yoel Hoffman.

97.54 Ram
199 3014   12-22-03   PKY
amo, Joshua Cooper.

o visible horizon
                          SDW

NO VISIBLE HORIZON

LeRoy Collins
Leon County Public Library
200 W. Park Avenue
Tallahassee, FL 32301

Sometimes the fear of dying is the cause of death.

—Seneca, *On Tranquility of Mind*

*In the middle of the
fifteenth century in Japan,
a strange tradition emerged.*

In the middle of the fifteenth century in Japan, a time when the kingdom was both at its most isolated and, to Japanese eyes, most perfect, a strange tradition emerged: composing haiku as you died, at the very moment of death. Perhaps it wasn't so surprising. Japanese culture had become obsessed with the relationship between life and art. There was an increasing belief that the two should never be separated, that a well-lived life was a work of art. Was it surprising that some Japanese poets wanted to try to weave the two together, to make a little tatami of life and art? What better time than at the moment of death? After a lifetime of study, could you be beautiful in three lines? Could you be perfect? Could you reduce it, all of it, your life, down to seventeen syllables?

> *Mame de iyo*
> *mi wa narawashi no*
> *kusa no tsuyu*

> *Farewell . . . I*
> *pass as all things do*
> *dew on the grass.*

So it all awaited you. Special inks were mixed. A brush of the rarest hair was prepared and left lying near your bed. The softest rice paper was fetched. All this lay waiting for your last moment. The Zen monks who collected the death poems looked for two virtues, two marks of beauty. The first was *aware*, a sense of the sadness of things passing, the way birds at dawn sing like mourners or cherry blossoms fall like tears in the spring. The second virtue was *mi-yabi*, an attempt to refine oneself. Everything about the poems—their sound, how they looked on the page—was meant to evoke this attempt at refinement, at compactness. So Basho, dead in early June 1807:

> *Tabi ni yande*
> *yume wa kareno o*
> *kakemeguru*
>
> *On a journey, ill:*
> *my dream goes wandering*
> *over withered fields.*

Or Cibuko, in the winter of 1788:

> *Yuku mizu to*
> *tomo ni suzushiku*
> *ishi kawa ya*
>
> *The running stream*
> *is cool . . . the pebbles*
> *underfoot.*

And, perfectly, Ozui, dead in January 1783:

> *Yo no hazuna*
> *Heirkiru ware mo*
> *Katachi nashi*

Still tied to this world
I cool off and lose
my form.

It is the kind of day to write poems about. The summer sky bleeds from soft robin's-egg blue at the horizon to deepest azure directly above. In between are a million more shades, as if God, restless and unsatisfied, has unloaded the full spectrum into the heavens. A few clouds hover harmlessly in the breeze-less sky, pulling weak shadows over the earth. It is a day to fall in love, to lie on the grass and listen to Louis Armstrong.

I am flying at the height of those clouds, 1,000 feet, and fast out of a dive: 200 miles an hour. To amuse myself I roll upside down and pass just above the clouds, dragging my tail in the vapor that steams upward from each, watching the reflection of my yellow plane. I pump the stick slightly to bump the nose up. The Extra 200, a German-built plane, is made for these aerial acrobatics the way a Porsche is made for the autobahn. I jam the stick to the left side of the cockpit, drawing the left wing ailerons up into the airstream, where they bite into the airflow and quickly pull the wing up and around, right side up, then inverted again. The Extra can come full around in less than a second, faster than you can say "roll." My shoulder and crotch belts dig into my skin as I float upside down. The steel ratchets that hold them tight grind at my hips. I stop the plane hard, exactly wings level and inverted. Sweat runs up from my chin and into my eyes.

I am going to pull through from here toward the ocean below me. Hold your hand out, palm up. Flip it over. Now arc it away from you and down. A split-S maneuver, de rigueur in competition aerobatics, the sport of precision flying. I fuss with the power a bit. I press the nose up for a second to make sure I am level. I glance out over the wing, squinting. Is it aligned with the horizon? As I set up I notice everything: the shudder and whir of the propeller, the twitch of my rudder in the slipstream, the stink of gasoline draining from the tank. What I don't notice is that I am cluelessly, stealthily losing altitude. I check and recheck my alignment, inverted for a good twenty seconds, ignoring my altimeter as it shows me leaching height. I am descending, unawares. I am about to start a maneuver that takes 800 feet from an altitude of 700 feet.

"Pssshhh." I pop the air out of my lungs and suck in a new breath as I start the pull. Almost immediately, my eyes begin to gray out as the blood rushes from my head. The g-meter creeps past seven. In the cockpit now I weigh seven times my weight, more than 1,000 pounds. I lose sight of the horizon and then my vision squeezes into a tunnel, as if I were peering through a paper-towel holder. I tuck my chin to my chest and close the back of my throat. I suck in on my abdominal muscles, trying to trap blood in my head and heart. I grunt, a hum of pain and stability. I am like a locked-in coma patient. My mind is alive in this useless hunk of a body. It is wonderful.

And then, in an instant no longer than it takes my brain to assemble a single neuron, I am terrified. I have seen from the angle of the sun and the sea below that I am too low. I can't tell how much I am off, but I know that even a foot is too much. Friends have died this way. "Aaargh." The breath shoots out of me in a horrified burst. In an instant my mind is cranking through the options. I don't have enough room to pull the maneuver through without putting more stress on the plane than it can handle, snapping the wings off. But I am too far along to roll the plane back upright. My options flip in front of me, shuffling cards, all bad. And then the thought comes to me, the one everyone always asks about. "If something happens up there, what will you think? Will you think the risks you took were worth the way your life ended? Will you be sad? Will you think of your family?" Here, on the last day of my life, in the last moment, I am writing a death poem with my plane. Now, with the water coming up at me at more than 200 miles per hour, what *am* I feeling? What am I thinking? I don't feel remorse or fear of death or even of pain. I don't think about my family or the life I am about to slam into pieces. What I am feeling in that one moment of truth is anger. Deep, profound anger.

"Shit," I think. "I've just killed myself."

*The best pilots in the world
compete in what is called
Unlimited Aerobatics.*

The best pilots in the world, perhaps sixty men and a dozen women, compete in what is called Unlimited Aerobatics. Of these sixty, a dozen or so occupy a little world of their own, the space of super-competitive pilots who devote the bulk of their lives to flying aerobatics. They put in hundreds of hours a year, stagger through blistering physical pain. There are few financial rewards. Though there have been attempts to make the sport into an aerial NASCAR, they have all failed. Unlimited pilots fly for joy and victory. Which makes it hard to say if it is noble or stupid that so many of them die.

Even the very best pilots, guys with tens of thousands of hours in planes, sometimes come up ten or twenty feet low on a loop. The Internet is filled with crash videos showing some "natural stick" air-show performer jamming happily into a maneuver in perfect form, with the best of intentions, and a hundred feet low. Sometimes on the video you can hear the announcer intoning away on a tinny, reverberating public address system as the disaster unspools: "And now he is coming in for his low-level pass. Out of the north and fast, here it comes, watch him. . . ." Silence. A suicide play-by-play. But there is an education in every one of these lethal mistakes. The flying life has always demanded a passage across the razor's edge. At any moment you could slip to the other side: a gas leak, weather, fire in the cockpit. You would beat at the flames with your hands, burning them. To no avail. Sometimes what made the risks horrible was that you could watch them play out in front of you; like a little opera, you could hear all the arias of your mistakes singing at you as the earth swam up. A chorus of your guilt followed you down. Occasionally you were able to get out and describe to others what this music had been like. But none of you ever stopped flying. That was the truly unthinkable thing.

But, my goodness, those final symphonies could be violent. Real Wagner stuff, the kind of music where it sounds like the orchestra is surely breaking something. Neil Williams, for instance, the champion British pilot. Never without the Navy blazer with the British Royal Flying Club seal stitched neatly over his heart. You could rip paper on the linear part in his Bryl-creamed hair. Neil was five-foot-six, lantern-jawed. A poster boy for furious flight. One day in the early 1970s he was test-flying a state-of-the-art Zlin 526 Aerobat, just knocking out a few figures to make sure everything was bolted on right. It was a sleek-looking plane, the Zlin, Czech built. The plane had jolted the flying world at the 1964 World Aerobatic Championships because it was the first plane to use the gyroscopic forces of the propeller in aerobatic maneuvers, turning itself into a form of out-of-control helicopter. The Czech plane was a challenge to the sangfroid of the British, who were used to building their own planes, thank you very much. But what could you do? The Zlin was a better plane than anything they made. So Williams set out to master it. Someone had done some small maintenance work to the British team Zlin. Williams took it for a quick test flight. The whole Eton-Oxford routine. *Back in a moment, chaps.* He did a couple of easy maneuvers and the plane felt fine. He's just pulling into a tight loop when he hears a bang and sees his left wing folding up toward the cockpit in the same way you might close your upraised palm into a fist.

What Neil didn't know was that his little Czech master-piece had a kind of cancer, a problem that caused the wing spars to split like a toothpick under high g loads. The spar is the long stick of metal that holds the wing to the airplane and, on the Zlin, if you punched it enough times, the spar began to shatter. It was a slow-motion affair. Williams's Zlin had been flying for years. The cancer was buried deep inside the wing, an impossible location to check. He had no idea what he was in for.

At this point Williams starts to think really fast. Actually thinking would be too slow. So he fires off on instinct alone, acting on pure faith. First he rolls the plane inverted and snaps the wing out like a one-way hinge. Imagine snapping out a carpet or a sheet. The wing cracks back into position just as he is finally upside down and leveled off. Williams takes a deep breath. Weird, to be sure, but probably salvageable. He starts to roll upright and . . . the wing starts to fold again. He tries a third time. The wing creaks upward, folding quickly now. So he rolls inverted again and begins thinking. No para-chute. He didn't bother to put one on. Routine flight, and all that. The engine hiccups. He's running out of gas. He tries rolling over yet again. No go. So as the fuel-starved engine begins to sputter, Williams starts an approach to landing at the airfield. Upside down. At any moment the left wing could just come flying off the plane, so he flies gently. He flies a short little traffic pattern. Upside down. Turns onto his final approach leg upside down, and, so low that he actually draws one wingtip through the grass, he fast rolls the plane back upright at the last possible moment and lands as the wing folds up. And walks away. He had pulled off a miracle at the very last second. You could imagine pilots flocking to that little line in the grass, the leaves still wingbrushed, like Hajjis to Mecca or pilgrims to some sighting of the Virgin Mary. That little line in the grass was *it*, they would say to each other, the visible border between miracle and martyrdom. The physical proof of man's faith.

Six years later Williams flew a WWII bomber head on into a mountain in Spain in bad weather, killing everyone on board, including his wife.

It is a commonplace of religious thought that there are two routes to enlightenment. One route is martyrdom; the other involves miracles. At first glance it is maybe surprising that the truth can be found with equal precision along a path of complete horror or by a route of pure wonder. But what martyrdom and miracles have in common is that each tastes of absolutely pure faith. As such, either offers a glimpse of the true world, the one that underlies our lives even if we cannot always see it. Sometimes this world, this true world, is so beautiful that it blinds the faithful and they can no longer tell which path they are on. Terror, for instance, becomes wonderful. Do you recall St. Perpetua, who in her eagerness to die drew the sword down upon her own neck?

In its early days, flying was a religion of sorts. It involved faith. It included both miracles and martyrdom. Largely this dangerous, wonderful magic has been bred out of flying now. Modern jetliners have no more in common with the miraculous early days of flight than most Sunday morning church services have in common with the murmuring *Te Deums* of fugitive Roman Christians. Flight is a miracle that has been domesticated into triviality. But out along its sharp edges, where test pilots crumple planes in midair or where aerobatic masters scream through figures and miss the ground by feet or inches or not at all, in those places where flying still draws blood, the chance for miracles remains. As does the risk of martyrdom. Either way, though, you are describing a route toward epiphany, toward total clarity. What you are talking about is the collection of impossible acts, the work of prophets and explorers and dreamers. And you discover that after you have collected a few of these acts, it is just possible that your faith becomes so strong that you stop caring about which path you are on. Martyrdom and miracles begin to look the same.

I had been flying for the better part of a decade. I had decided at some point in college that I wanted to be an astronaut. I had a curiosity about the world we share and about the things outside of it that we cannot see. Partly this was a love of math and physics and flying. There was a broken heart thrown in there too, and the appealing idea of distances so vast. My plan was to join the Marine Corps as a pilot, get my Ph.D. in physics, and then just fly. I passed through the paperwork. The eyes, thank God, better than okay. I thought I had best be sure I fit the flying too. Straight and level in a Cessna was one thing. Upside down was something else. So I found my way to an aerobatics school. It was wonderful, instantly, like your first glimpse of Paris in the rain at night. The lights come through the mist. The Marines wanted ten years of my life in exchange for time in their jets and somehow, even at twenty-two, I could see this was too much. We talked around the various details. No one would really stay that long, the sergeant told me. He was my height, twice my weight with muscles. *Pilots were already being let go early from their contracts.* But the decade terrified me. It scared the astronaut right out of my plans. I chose another, less expensive life.

The flying remained. The aerobatics grew. I wasn't doing it often, ten hours in a good year. But it had an outsized place in my soul. At night I would dream of myself upside down over a river landscape, the liberation so vivid that it occasionally woke me. In meetings I would find my hand working an imaginary control stick and my feet dancing on rudders. *Yes, of course, I'll get on that right away.* Meanwhile, the chill beauty of an inverted plane pulling up hard through thin winter air fortified me. So one winter day I decided that the time had come to go from a hobbyist aerobatic pilot to a serious competitive aerobatic pilot. I wanted to finish among the top ten pilots in my division at U.S. Nationals, nine months away. I wanted to make a refinement of myself.

. . .

I've moved around a bit and in every new town there is a ritual I have to go through before I can rent a plane from the local flight school. They make me ride with a flight instructor, an insurance check-ride. *Can he land the thing in one piece?* And even if I haven't been up for months, I can move the plane around the sky exactly as I wish. It is like sitting down at a piano again after years and finding your technique still intact, the sound only slightly less bright. I would open with a high performance takeoff, lifting the plane just a few feet off the runway and leveling there to build speed. I'd draw the landing gear up as the first three-quarters of the runway disappeared behind us, the plane buzzing along at treetop height, throttle firewalled. Then a sharp tug back on the controls, abruptly pulling up into a fast climb out. Right foot pressed slightly onto the rudder to offset the corkscrewing propeller slipstream, feeling the plane move sideways and back on line. Hand down fast to the flaps, bringing them up with a flick. A crisp turn out of the traffic pattern. From the instructor, invariably, "Nice." For whatever reason I have always been completely sure in the cockpit. There are other places where my confidence deserts me. Like other men, I am vulnerable. But any plane does as I ask.

I had many things I needed to do, but they could be reduced. I had to buy a plane and then learn to fly it. A top ten finish at Nationals was an arrogant and ambitious goal. Even at the introductory level of competition I would be flying against pilots who had hundreds of hours of aerobatic time in their logbooks, decades of experience. I had never flown a single contest. Never performed more than idle figures. In aerobatics experience is everything, an irreplaceable currency. Under the press of a half-dozen g's or screaming along at 250 miles an hour while pointed earthward there is no time for on-the-spot learning. Making a national champion is considered a decade's work. The sport is too fast and too precise and too demanding to move much faster.

In Russia, aerobatic pilots sometimes train by sitting in their cockpits for hours flying routines without taking off. The pilots scream and grunt through the figures as if they are in the air. Coaches stand next to the parked planes and shout at the pilots, they rattle the wings, anything to increase the stress. The pilots are expected to climb out of the cockpit wet with sweat. They are expected to feel the flight in their nerves, to ascend inside their own brains. They have to ignore the absurd odds and the objectively insane nature of what they are doing. Great aerobatic flight is not just about keeping the fear and terror away. To fly well, to fly really well and to live, you have to operate past the limits of your ability, over the edge of your own confidence. As you train, the things you do in your plane carry you beyond the limits of what you thought possible. Sometimes, in order to win you have to press past what the engineers or your own body insists is possible. The physical evidence of this departure from the land of the possible is immediate. You can feel the plane creak or buffet or twist when it is unhappy or worried. Your own body begins to rebel, first with pain, then nausea, then blackout. But the physical evidence is irrelevant in a way. It's like what's left behind at a murder scene. The physical evidence is just a set of clues. It offers no hint of a motive.

For truly great pilots, the plane is simply an accouterment and the human body is an inconvenience. You fly your brain. Your brain flies the plane. This was the place I wanted to go, a field where the line between the physical and the mental was dissolved by pure speed and crushed by many times the force of gravity. A place of pure faith.

Imagine walking through a minefield. Imagine *enjoying* it. "The problem with aerobatics is that it is very emotionally stressful," Sergei Boriak explains to me one night over a beer. Boriak is a former Soviet champion. He still looks like the paratrooper he once was, his small body muscled like an expensive side of beef, his thinning hair slicked back over his head. He moves with a ballerina's precision, the same robot-like efficiency that first drew the Soviet talent spotters to him decades ago. "This one could be a champion," they speculated. We are sitting on a verandah overlooking a lake in deep west Texas, where Sergei has spent his day refining the technique of two of the best American pilots. Boriak makes his living now coaching Western pilots, sharing the fruits of decades of Soviet research into how you can make men do impossible, painful, perfect things in airplanes. Boriak's brutal English mimics his flying style. "Aerobatics ees stressful because you are not on ground. This ees feerst emotional stress." Of course this is the kick too. You are in the sky, upside down, pushing through some figure as the wings chuckle with the stress, flirting with a stall. After a while you start to believe you belong up here, your faith is so strong. And that's the moment you get into trouble. The second you think you really were born to fly, you'll be taught that man was born, one way or another, to be on the ground. The miracle of physics and engineering that has put you aloft is not enough to keep you there if you make a mistake.

"To guide planes through the air you have to worry," Boriak continues, sucking on a beer as powerboats shoot past on the lake below. "Physically, you are stressed because it is not one-g up there. There it is like someone compressing your body for eighteen minutes and doing it in the air in a plane that you will have to land safely." Few aerobatic pilots can practice effectively for longer than twenty minutes at a crack. Their bodies begin to give up. Their hands shake, they lose their eyesight, g-driven headaches begin pushing on their temples. Boriak is silent for a minute. The pink Texas sunset gathers incongruously into the corners of his face. "You should be uneasy."

Boriak has a test for me. On a spring morning, early in our relationship, he takes me out to the cockpit of his red-on-white SU-29, an unforgiving two-place Soviet aerobatic plane. It is a two-part test and though they are unstated, I know the elements in my head: we are going flying for the first time and he wants to know will I get sick and will I be afraid? As I strap on my borrowed parachute and lash myself into the front cockpit, I wonder too. I have asked Sergei to be my coach, and if he is going to be one of my guides, I have to show that I belong in his world. Both of these things will be out of my control. If I am sick, my body will make it so. If I am terrified, the sting will come from a part of my brain that I won't be able to shut off. This is the ultimate macho endgame. It is a test to see what you are made of, a test that you cannot study for or cheat on. Either nausea and terror or something, anything else. Fail or pass.

Boriak triggers the small air-compressor that fires like a gun to start the Sukhoi engine. "Boom." The cockpit rattles as the radial engine kicks into uneven life, a few cylinders missing. "What do you want to do?" I ask him over the intercom, feeling out what may lie ahead. "You fly," he shouts back. "Your plane. We do what you want to do. Nothing else." I feel a bit of relief, perhaps this won't be what I expected. I glance at my watch as we take off. 10:45. If I am lucky, this will all be over by 11:00. It is a terrible attitude.

We are in the air and after making a few sharp turns to ensure the area underneath us is clear, I level off at 3,000 feet. I begin easing the plane back into a gentle stall. I want to get a sense of how she flies and one of the best ways to do this is to slow down to the point where the wing doesn't have enough air moving over it to keep flying. The plane will waddle and grunt into the stall, the engine backfiring, but in her gentle fury I'll have a sense of how and why she likes to move. It is like feeling up a girl during a slow dance, an easy way to see where you can put your hands and how this mystery is likely to react. So I pull the power back and nestle the stick up against my belly, bringing the nose up. And as the speed bleeds off we settle down into a stall. The right wing starts to fall away. I quickly pick it back up with opposite rudder. I calmly pop the nose down to pick up airspeed and stop the stall. We are flying again. The whole experience is very benign, almost no g's pulled.

"Goot. Let me have plane for moment." From the back seat, Boriak sounds different now. Happy, childish almost. "You must have plane trimmed just right to fly." The airplane's trim is a small control that only Sergei can reach, a kind of power-steering that helps keep the stick-pressures from getting out of hand. I begin to sock this away as lesson number one from Sergei: "Always trim plane" when suddenly the sky is torn away from me. Sergei slams the stick forward and in an instant we are screaming earthward on a pure vertical line. The power is full forward, accelerating us from a gentle cruising speed to nearly 250 miles an hour. We are losing more than 5,000 feet a minute. Now 7,000. Then down so fast the meter runs out of room. I can make out branches on the trees below. I can see leaves. At 300 feet, Boriak slams the stick back, pulling us to level flight with a tug that puts six times the force of gravity on our bodies and throws us into our seats with a thud. I relax for a moment. Mistake. Wham, Boriak is back on the stick hard, cranking us straight back up into the sky at about seven g's. Aerobatics on the very edge looks graceful from the outside. This is the real story: an explosion of violence, the stick slammed from side to side as the airplane screams.

Boriak sets the nose on a vertical upline with a tiny push, just enough to make the plane hold zero-g for a second. I float in the cockpit, a little loose in my harness, as he slams the stick to the right and we begin twisting up through the sky. The airspeed is slowly bleeding off and, as the plane teeters on the edge of a stall, Boriak taps us over into a dive and we are screaming earthward again. Twenty-one thousand feet per minute. Straight down.

I am looking outside the cockpit during all of this. The earth spools up and down through the canopy, sometimes above, sometimes below, sometimes racing up. A confused window. After a few of these hard pull maneuvers, I begin to gray out as the blood rushes from my head and, at certain moments, I can see little more than a dim tunnel of light ahead of me. With my visibility outside reduced, I begin to look inside. I find that I don't feel the least bit sick. There is no nausea or discomfort. And I find that as the ground races up at us, as Boriak whips the Sukhoi around the sky with forces that would pull an ordinary airplane apart, that I feel no fear. I look for the fear in myself like you might look for lost keys or a misplaced wallet. "Surely," I think, "it is here somewhere." But it is nowhere to be found. We are racing down again. Wham! Boriak pulls us flat. Wham! He cranks us back into the sky and we are on our backs with the earth racing away. Turbulence shakes the plane as we begin to stall and slip backward. The Texas sun burns at my face. We teeter over the top of the line. In this furious rummage of my soul, I have found no fear and, amazingly, a tiny hint of real pleasure. Bam! We are level again, 300 feet, 250 miles an hour. "Okay," Sergei says, the self-satisfied smile trickling through the intercom. "Plane trimmed. All yours. How you feel?" It is 11:00. I am ready to learn to fly.

Kirby Chambliss

was thinking.

Kirby Chambliss was thinking. There was a lot to think about. He paced the whole impossible act off in his head. For a moment he ran the flight down as if he were perusing a checklist: get in the airplane, jerk free of the runway, accelerate to 170 miles an hour or so, and fly through a hole in a cliff. You had to stop and scratch your head at that last item. *Fly through a hole in a cliff.* He could already hear the roar of the 150,000 Chinese who were gathered for the spectacle. They stretched from the runway here all the way out to the hole itself. Flying planes through cliffs was big news in China, a big act of faith. The Chinese called the hole Heaven's Gate, but it wasn't really much of a gate. It wasn't some thin two-dimensional thing you could just pop through, like the drill team at homecoming grin-popping through a piece of painted paper. No, the hole was a tunnel. A 150-foot-long rock tube screwed out of a ropy red sandstone cliff face by millennia of erosion. It was ninety feet wide at one point. Fifteen planes, flying through one after another. Fifteen accidents waiting to happen, one after another. Live on Chinese television. Heaven's gate? Maybe. Act of faith? For sure.

Kirby was standing on a hot, black-tarred runway about five miles from the hole. There was a dervish of a breeze, lightly tickling his brown-blond surfer's cut from every corner of the compass. He was a center of attention; the Chinese were riveted by him, a high priest of American aerobatics. Everything about him said it: the blond hair, the blue eyes, the aw-shucks gait that syncopated his spare six-foot frame as he paced around his plane. Kirby looked like he had just peeled himself off of some Southern California beach, kicked off his flip-flops, and slipped into a parachute. He was a fast pilot, he flew aerobatics with razored precision, but personally nothing keyed him up. He could sit in the plane and do extreme things because his mind was more or less beach-ready at any moment. You could almost hear him humming to himself as he flew. He was going to get bumped around on this flight, he knew. So what? The approach to the hole would be speckled with little eddies of air, invisible until they started juggling his 1,300-pound plane like a paint mixer. Kirby's plane was thirty feet from wingtip to wingtip. A bad bump could jam him into the rock before he had time to recover.

Then there were the Chinese. Jesus, they were everywhere. One hundred thousand at the airfield alone. Another 50,000 packed along the sides of the cliff near the hole, all fodder for a flying prop or crashing plane. The seating was strictly old-school Commie, with the most powerful officials jammed right up against the front of the hole smiling and chattering as they slurped down mao-tais from canteens. One small mistake, one unfortunate gust, and Kirby would smash right into them, using several dozen local apparatchiks to absorb the screaming shock of his plane. Kirby figured he'd walk away from any problem. But he didn't think he'd walk very far from that problem. Not with 150,000 (less a few dozen) pissed-off Chinese right there.

To be totally honest, Kirby *was* a little troubled. Not by the chance of a wreck, though. That was never enough to stop the humming. Not here, not back home in Arizona, not during the summer a few years back when a friend had been killed every single weekend, a year when he could almost set his watch by the bad-news Sunday night calls. You could burn yourself up with worry if you wanted. What was the point? No, what was itching at Kirby this morning was the problem of what the hell he was going to do *inside* the hole. It wasn't enough to take three weeks off from his job hauling tourists and businessmen and families and mail for an American airline to drag his ass all the way to China, just to fly straight-and-level through a hole. That was like trivial flight-instructor stuff to him, something a kid back in Phoenix might try in a Cessna after one too many Tecates. Kirby Chambliss was a high priest of aerobatic flight. His act-of-faith needed to be extraordinary. So, as he stood on the runway, staring through acrid smog in the general direction of the hole in the rock (it was over there, right?) what perplexed him was this: should he roll through the hole, cranking the plane around in an elegant twist as the rock spooled by all around him? Should he loop into the hole? Or what about a snap roll, a kind of super-violent horizontal spin? A normal human being, sitting in Kirby's brain watching these thoughts play out, might phrase the question as: how can I take something dangerous and make it into a fucking paragon of danger? How can I make the Chinese go home, look up danger in their little Red dictionaries, and see my face smiling back? This was going to be on live TV, right?

Ten-million-plus Chinese watching? They needed to know what he knew. There was no better pilot.

What, he wondered, would Jurgis do?

Kirby looked over at Jurgis Kayris, standing near his Russian-built aerobatic plane. Jurgis was an aeronautical prodigy who had helped pencil out the design of the Sukhoi back when he was the top cock of the Soviet team. He was older now, past forty, and an even craftier stick. In Vilnius, Lithuania, one weekend he had flown his plane under ten bridges in a row. Upside down. It was a guerrilla prank; even the government didn't know it was coming. They had tried to act angry. The local police had fined him for "illegal advertising" since his plane was plastered with cigarette logos. But to bust him for the flying? No one would seriously consider it. Jurgis was a national treasure. People talked about him running for president some day. "Every pilot has his own personal limits," one European writer observed after the bridge stunt. "For Jurgis, flying inverted with his tail fin six inches off the water is his personal limit. 'I'm unable to go any lower,' he said." You could almost hear the smirk. But six inches really was Jurgis's limit. And Kirby's? Maybe six inches was too high? At competitions, awed pilots would point to the little marks running up along the tail of Chambliss's plane, places where he had scraped it against the runway pulling up into vertical maneuvers, they gossiped. The nicks said: "My personal limit is zero inches. I am unable to go any lower."

Lined up back along the runway were another dozen wide-winged, over-engined aerobatic planes, Russian-built Sukhois and Yaks, Czech-made Zlins, a German Extra, and

Kirby's Edge 540. The names sounded great, little haiku of power and grace. Next to them all, pilots laughing and chattering in a half-dozen languages, all probably thinking along the same lines as Kirby. Roll? Snap? Loop? Zero-inch pilots one and all. But even here, even at the summit of competitive flying, there was a hierarchy, a constant compulsive contest to see who was the best. Just to get here you had to be willing to never back off the edge. The minute you did you became a Cessna driver, you gave up your claim to the brotherhood. But to stay on the edge? That was to hold on to what was magical about flight, to say something about man and machine, about fate and faith. Look at Martin Stahalik over there by his plane.

An absolute aerial genius, Picasso of the skies. An athletic six-footer with dark hair he brushed down in a Little Caesar cut, Stahalik was a past master of risk and recovery. Once, deep into a competition sequence, the prop on his plane had screamed right off the engine, snapped loose like a coffee-stick. (Imagine what those forces did to the man!) And as the prop tumbled to the ground below him, as his plane nearly shook itself apart, Stahalik shut down the engine, finished the figure, drove the plane back onto the runway and, incidentally, won the contest. He'd be dead a year after this China adventure, spun into the soft summer grass of an airfield near Amsterdam, the wrong side of the zero-inch limit.

This was standard aerobatics. Competence wasn't insurance against death. Kind of the opposite. The better you were, the more extreme your flying had to be. Getting better just gave you more chances to kill yourself. There was simply no way to avoid the math. It caught everyone eventually. One way or another you would have to look at an ultimate mistake from your cockpit. Just how costly that mistake was going to be, well, who knew? The sport was merciless that way. Take the first world-class U.S. aerobatic team, circa 1960: Hal Krier, Art Scholl, Bob Herendeen, Charlie Hillard. Some of the best pilots America had ever produced. Yeager-class pilots, men made to fly in the same way most people are made to eat and breathe. The kind of guys who could land propless planes too, just like Stahalik. Guys who grew up flying, who soloed planes when they were twelve, who amassed tens of thousands of hours of flight time. Would the flying take one or two of them in its random violence? Was 50 percent too much interest to ask for a life spent in the skies doing wonderful things? No. Airplanes killed every fucking one of them.

That was the price. Extreme flight was a way of life, in competition or airshows or even just flying in shitty weather, confident that you didn't need more than fifty feet of forward visibility to land safely . . . until some idiot strung a treetop-high power line across the road you were following. You couldn't escape it. You might try to be a reasonable pilot, to avoid the risks. But they would find you. Over some mountain, flying wingtip to wingtip with a friend on the way back from a competition. In clouds. Without instruments. The macho instinct was like anger. It surged in you. Later, after you landed, you might say, "What the fuck did I just do?" But you would do it again. It was, in truth, like being an addict. And it was wonderful, every second. Even the last one.

Competition aerobatics itself is a kind of aerial ice skating, with an international panel of judges who grade each figure. But this isn't ice skating, of course. When was the last time Kristy Yamaguchi burst into flames in the middle of a salchow? No one had ever been killed at a U.S. competition. Bailouts, sure. But no deaths in the United States. Thank God for that, the grandfathers of the sport, the old white-haired guys on the sidelines of competitions, would say to one another. A competition was just too intense to permit the kind of aerial fucking around that would kill you. You came to a competition to win, and that meant extreme caution even along the very edge of what was recoverable. The old white-haired guys at the contests held on to this as a proof of the sport's overall safety. Which would have been okay except for the fact that the old white-haired guys were *the survivors*. They collected dead friends the way most codgers collect golf tees. Between 600 and 800 pilots fly some kind of aerobatics during a year. In a bad year fifteen to twenty end up on the wrong side of the zero-inch limit. One in thirty, one in forty dead.

What was weird about the whole thing, what puzzled even the old guys, was that the sport seemed to be as hungry to kill good pilots as bad. Take the Unlimited jocks like Kirby. The name said it all: no limits. You did everything in a plane that was possible. To fly Unlimited Aerobatics you had to be so deeply familiar with your plane that everything seemed recoverable. Whoa! There goes the prop. No problem. It takes years to get that sort of control, to build the confidence that comes with it. And to hold on to that confidence as you hit the turbulence of dead friends and your own near misses? That doesn't take years. That is innate. You either do it or not.

No sport on earth kills more of its participants. One minute you are waxing about the zero-inch limit. The next you are eating it. A medical or personal or mechanical fluff melts your illusions like a fog, and it does it all at once. Maybe one spark plug misfires at the top of a loop. At the wrong moment that can be enough. Between every flight in China, Martin Stahalik and his mechanic pulled every goddamned spark plug from his engine (eighteen of them), cleaned them like crown jewels on coronation day, and put them back in place. He was taking no chances, right? His plugs were probably spotless when he cratered in Amsterdam. On hangar walls around the United States you'll find an old photo of a biplane that some pilot has smashed into a tree. It has this hortatory caption: "Aviation is not inherently dangerous. But to an even greater extent than the sea, it is terribly unforgiving of any carelessness, incapacity or neglect."

Kirby and the other aces were in China for a paid aerobatics competition. Someone, probably at China TV, had a thought: while the guys are here, why not run 'em through Heaven's Gate? The local aviation authorities loved the idea right away. Great for China, showing the whole country how advanced their aviation system was by, uh, having foreign pilots fly through a hole in a rock! Possibly some would crash. Still, good for China, right? Good TV, at least. Kirby thought this rattling love of spectacle was one of the great things about Asia. It resonated with his own love of a good show, his own itch to put one on for his audience. In the States, every time you wanted to go upside down in a plane you had to consider a phone book of FAA rules. The Feds specified how many degrees of wing-bank you were allowed before you were considered to be flying aerobatics, how far you could move the nose. It was like having your mom on board. But in Asia, local aviation authorities were just so fucking slack-jawed that anyone would do this shit that it never occurred to them to regulate it, to say nothing of stopping it. In Japan, Kirby had flown a whole routine pretty much on top of a crowd. Necks cracked back, several thousand Japanese had cheered as Kirby looped, rolled, and dove the plane right at them. "Aaah!" Kirby liked to say, imitating the way the Japanese had scurried away in horror from his descending plane. In the United States, the FAA set up designated "dead lines" at air shows well away from crowds. Fly over the dead line, lose your flight ticket. In the United States you could wait five years before the FAA cleared you across their paperwork river and into the Promised Land known as ground-level aerobatics. In Japan you could slink off a plane at Narita in the morning and be cranking ten g's over a Tokyo crowd by mid-afternoon.

What would Jurgis do? Kirby looked down the flight line. What would they all do? There was Victor Chemal, surely among the best pilots of them all, plotting out his routine. Victor looked as if he belonged on a Hungarian postage stamp. Handsome, with a graying pre-WWI mustache, he was known for a gambler's touch on the stick, a willingness to wait until just the last moment before moving his plane. Next to Victor was Boriak, the former Soviet champion, now in his late forties. Boriak was engaged in a typical activity, banging his Sukhoi back into working order. While most aerobatic planes are built with the delicate precision of Formula One race cars, the Sukhois were famous for being built by the Russians in the same way they built tanks. "Ees traktor," Boriak would say as he worked the engine over. With a hammer. He had been a test pilot on the Suk before he was twenty-five. Someone had installed a camera in Sergei's cockpit here and the pilots had already seen the TV images of handsome Sergei, straining under high-g loads, pushing his cheeks out and knitting his brow hard to hold the blood in his brain as he chunked the plane through one tight figure after another. He looked like a monkey with a headset. The monkey flew here representing Kazakhstan.

Kirby admired the Sukhoi as a plane, the way a Corvette owner might see some good points about a Mustang. The Suk could climb fast. But it was a pig, he thought, heavy and slow to roll. Kirby's plane was an Edge 540, the best aerobatic plane ever made in the United States. During the 1970s and 1980s the United States had produced the finest aerobatic mounts in the world, little two-wing Pitts biplanes made of wood and fabric. But in the early 1990s single-wing planes made from extra-light and extra-strong composites began edging the Pitts out of competitions. The new planes could handle higher g-loads too, which ostensibly made them safer. In fact, pilots just took the new g-limits as an excuse to fly harder. The judges loved the new, tight flying. The Pitts became a relic, replaced by the French-made CAPs and Russian Suks.

The first credible threat to European dominance was

Kirby's Edge, made of light carbon fiber and hung with a 300 horsepower engine and a high-torque propeller. The plane was built around a wing that allowed it to fly as well upside down as right side up, to roll at 540 degrees a second. It could climb at better than 5,000 feet per minute and could pull into a vertical line and fly straight up for 3,000 feet before tumbling away earthward, spent like a racehorse. That agility, with an admixture of pure speed, made the Edge ideal for aerobatics. Jet planes, moving at 300 or 400 miles an hour, take too much space in the sky for aerobatics. Planes like the Edge were a compromise, suited to maneuver in the 3,300-foot-square cube that marks the outline of an aerobatic "box."

There were an awful lot of curious Chinese around his plane, Kirby noticed. Some of them were taking notes. Well, hell, he thought, there wasn't too much for them to learn from looking. The Edge kept most of its secrets buried in the formulas that produced the composite parts and the mathematical models that explained the supercritical wing. There was no high-tech gear in the cockpit that was worth stealing. Who needed the extra weight? Gyros? Artificial horizons? Ten pounds! Pilots were dieting to boost their climb rates.

Heaven's Gate. A long way from home in Arizona, to be sure. Kirby still flew occasionally for the airline these days, when his schedule allowed it, but mostly his life was aerobatics. Though he was one of the company's most senior captains, there was no great seduction in the heavy metal of the Boeings. "Even if

I won the lotto, I'd stick around," guys at work would say to each other, sitting up front in the planes with the autopilot on, reading *Yachting* or *Field and Stream* or some other magazine related to a hobby that made you fatter. They liked this life. "If I wanted to fly a seven-three-seven I'd buy one," Kirby said of his imagined post-lotto life. A 747? Fly for fourteen hours at a whack? *I don't think so.* Kirby's real flying was now done in seven-minute chunks, the seven hard minutes of an Unlimited aerobatic routine.

But the Boeings had brought good things to Kirby. The house in the desert an hour south of Phoenix. Two landing strips there and a private box marked out on the ground for Kirby to practice. The fabulous-looking wife, a stewardess. A swimming pool plunked down right under the aerobatic box so Kirby's flying buddies could soak while he twisted and pulled over their heads. And the Boeings brought a lifestyle that let Kirby take the time he needed to keep a fingertip feel for the airplane. Even a week away from the plane and it all felt different, rocky, not quite right.

Kirby had picked up the aerobatics as a result of his first big-time flying gig, driving a Cessna Citation jet for La Quinta Inns. His job was to ferry teams of accountants around on surprise audits to unsuspecting La Quinta managers. "Can we see your books please?" If you looked closely, you could see the managers begin to moisten. Kirby was the only copilot on a three-person flight staff. The captains split the duties three days and two. Kirby flew five. Whenever the plane moved, he was on it. He was twenty. The job had perks. Kirby could stay at any La Quinta, though he and the other pilots registered under fake names, since nervous managers had started distributing lists of the pilots' names as an audit early-warning system. If "Kirby Chambliss" had checked into a La Quinta in Omaha, La Quinta phones would be ringing as far away as Otumwa.

Another perk was the jet time. Kirby was putting about a hundred hours a month into his logbook, triple what he'd see in his airline job. That let him log enough jet time in two years to land the job flying heavy metal. He had selected the airline because it was one of only four that flew 737s, a plane with no flight-engineer position. FEs were the guys who sat *behind* the pilots and wrote down things like what the oil pressure was doing every five minutes. FEs sat in the cockpits of 747s, 727s, DC-10s, L-1011s for about three years before ever getting to so much as taxi a plane. The Boeing 737 had just two slots up front, both for pilots. Perfect for Kirby. No backseat for him. Everyone got laid, if you know what I mean.

Kirby's boss back at La Quinta was a guy named Jerry Anderson. Jerry decided that maybe it wasn't such a bad idea for his pilots to be upside down every now and then. So the company paid for five hours of aerobatics every year. Duane Cole, an American aerobatics legend, would haul down to San Antonio and teach them a few tricks in an old Decathlon. Imagine finding your life's work in an immediate flash, like getting a mental telegram saying THIS IS WHAT YOU ARE TO DO. The first time Duane drove the little Decathlon wings past vertical, Kirby was done for. In a way it was the kind of distraction you didn't want. But you couldn't stop yourself. After he went to work at the airline, he was one excited dude. He was twenty-four, surrounded by beautiful flight attendants. (That was key because he'd been flying with guys for two years.) He had this super attitude for a pilot. His dream had come true. And then one day, driving back from the airport, his brain started up on him. "Now what?" He bought an aerobatic plane. Within a year the job became an inconvenience.

The pilots at work didn't want to talk much about the aerobatics. Chambliss was a check-airman, meaning he was responsible for giving proficiency checks to his fellow pilots every six months. Everyone at the line knew Kirby had won the 1998 U.S. National Aerobatic Championships. They knew he was among the best in the world. But there wasn't a lot of ass-slapping about the aerobatics. Didn't *everyone* want to fly aerobatics?

There are, Kirby was discovering, two kinds of guys—still just a few women—in the cockpits of those Boeings. Some of them loved everything about flight, dreamed of takeoffs when they went to bed at night, savored landings like wines. And then there were the bus drivers. There were other divisions too. The split, for instance, between civilian-trained pilots and the ex-military jocks. The civilian flyers, who had laddered their way up through flight schools and then jobs like the one Kirby had in his teens flying auto parts through Texas nights, tended to be more interested in aerobatics. The military guys rarely ventured past a macho nibble or two. "How many g's you pull?" they'd ask casually. And then they'd balk at the answer. "No way anyone pulls ten g's and walks away. And ten *negative* g's. Not happening." Negative g's were impossible in fighter jets, which require the constant force of gravity in order to keep fuel flowing. But it did happen. Every flight for Kirby. It was right there on his g-meter. Or it would have been on the g-meter if Kirby hadn't torn his out because after a while he decided he just didn't want to know how many g's he was pulling. Negative g's were what happened when you pushed the plane around instead of pulling, the force of gravity trying to throw you out of your seat instead of keeping you in it. With positive g's, the blood rushed from your head. With negative g's it rushed in, often painfully. The planes are designed for the stress. In Kirby's Edge, you could go from +10 to -10 for as long as your body could take it. After a good flight Kirby would step out of his plane covered in sweat, maybe shaking slightly, his eyes a little red. He could drop a dozen pounds in a hard week of training. After a good flight the military guys could get out of their F-16s and go home without a shower. No wonder they weren't interested.

Learning to fly aerobatics requires a walk away from the world of traditional flight training. The average flying student, soldiering toward a license in a Cessna, rarely sees anything that resembles aerobatics. The initial impression of aerobatics—scary and a little out of control—is enough to take it off the agendas of most flight schools. The retired schoolteachers who populate most flight schools, or the young kids trying to build hours toward an airline job, aren't inclined to risk their planes. I tried to get a dozen teachers to show me a spin when I was learning to fly. None would oblige. Wisely, I think now. They probably could not have reliably recovered.

There's a cost to this ignorance. It comes later, when a pilot suddenly finds himself upside down in the clouds or low-and-slow on final approach. Then the unfamiliarity with how the plane flies outside a limited envelope becomes fatal. Unusual Attitudes, as the FAA calls them, are ghoulish things. They strike at bad moments, by which I mean close to the ground. Their basic aerodynamics demand a different language of flight. The instincts that would save you in many situations can kill you in an unusual attitude. A Cessna pilot on final approach at a big airport slips in behind a 747 to land, for example. A wingtip vortex from the Boeing, essentially a whirlwind, grabs the tiny plane and snaps it over on its back. The vortex is twisting at about 300 degrees a second. The roll-rate on the small plane is about 100 degrees a second. It is badly outclassed. Now our pilot is upside down. His first instinct, as demonstrated to proficiency by many dead pilots, is to pull back on the stick, trying to bring the plane through a little half-loop. He pulls hard. But he never has enough altitude. As the ground rushes up, he pulls harder. Pieces of the plane, now breaking apart under the g-load, rain down like cracker crumbs. The pull is an instinct. Without training to do the right thing, to lean hard forward and force the plane to roll upright, it is a suicidal reaction.

Kirby had come to understand that every pilot has an envelope that describes what he's willing to do in a plane. And most pilots have a damn small envelope. There's nothing wrong with that, of course. But for pilots who have huge envelopes, the narrow envelopes are a puzzle. One aerobatic pilot, who makes his living at an airline, recalls a flight in his early days as a copilot with a captain whose envelope included about 5 degrees of wing bank. This made for some very weird flights. The captain was afraid of his plane. But that could kill you too. Motorcycle racers called it target-fixation. You stare at the thing you want to avoid and, inevitably, you crater right into it. One afternoon, as this captain brought a jet in for landing, his fear almost killed a whole planeful of folks. To slow down a passenger jet for landing, engineers have designed all kinds of stuff to throw into the airflow: flaps, spoilers, air brakes. But at slow speed all these devices can change the turn and roll characteristics of the plane. Beyond a certain angle of bank, the plane can accelerate its roll sharply. It's as if you were turning your car and when you cranked the steering wheel past 20 degrees it had a hundred times the effect. At several hundred miles an hour and just thousands of feet above the ground this kind of snatch can be dangerous. One day, at about 3,000 feet, with his aerobatic-trained co-pilot watching, Captain Terror gently banked his usual 5 degrees to line up with the runway. But because he had mis-calculated for wind or something, he was turning too gently. Slowly he added more and more bank until, suddenly, the plane hit the roll acceleration point and began slipping through 20, 25, 30, 35 degrees of bank. Sitting in the left seat, where the captain always sits on airliners, he just froze as the wing started dropping earthward. He was so far outside his envelope he did not know what to do, even though all that was required was to simply turn the plane the opposite direction. It was like he had been dropped on Mars. Finally, he figured out what his amused copilot had been thinking all along: put in opposite controls.

Few pilots are born with perfect instincts. Kirby recalls going out in his pre-aerobatic days as a flight instructor and leading his students through stall sequences. Handled badly, a stall causes the wing of the plane to drop. Handled really badly that wing-drop can turn into a spin. *Jesus!* Kriby would think as the plane fell. *I have no idea how to get this airplane out of a spin.* Never push the rudder all the way in, he told himself. You didn't know what is going to happen.

Yet the more Kirby flew, the more he thought he did know what was going to happen. He could hear the plane. On good days, he could even tell by the sound of the wind going past the wings what was going to happen next. And so he started to develop a, well, what's the right word for it? Confidence? No, that's not quite solid enough. Kirby just started to know in every nerve that he wasn't going to crash his plane, at least not while he was able to control it. He was learning, especially from his mistakes. After nearly two decades of flying, Kirby thought you could freeze frame the plane at any moment and he could get from there to the ground safely. It wasn't arrogance—okay, maybe there was a little of that—but it was more like a kind of fusion of time and talent. I don't worry, he said like a mantra. His wife, Kellie? *She can't worry all the time, it gets tiring.* "That's not to say that I won't make a mistake. But I worry more about something breaking." It was like when they set off the atomic bomb in the New Mexican desert and the heat turned the sand to glass. The more Kirby flew the more the blaze of his confidence melted the sands of his doubts into something else altogether.

Once Kirby was practicing a routine that involved a rolling vertical climb, essentially a line straight up with lots of rolls as you go. In particular, this sequence required that he fly straight up and do a two-point roll, a roll that would stop after 180 degrees for a fraction of a second before continuing on to finish the complete 360 degrees. Kirby pulled hard to vertical. He jammed the stick left to start the roll. It snapped off in his hand.

"Fuuuuck."

"Well," he thought, "at least I'm going up." That was a good start. Flying the plane with the nub of the fractured stick, Kirby made it back to the ground. Sort of like driving a car with the parking brake, but no steering wheel. At 200 miles an hour. Kirby has also snapped the tail off of a biplane. He landed on a runway that just happened to be right below him. In 1998, he pulled so hard during the World Championships in France that he sheared clean through a three-quarter-inch steel tube in the front of his Edge. He landed fine that time too. "I've heard for years from people that I'm going to die in an airplane," Kirby said. *You know you can die tomorrow doing this*, he said to himself. "There is a sense that if you fly a certain way—aggressive— you're going to die. The guy I hear that about is a guy coming up right now, he flies aggressive. And low. And someone was saying he's going to die. And I said, 'Come on. We've heard that for years. They said it about me.'" A lot of times, Kirby thought, people said that because they didn't want to fly that way themselves. "They're going to have to," he said, "if they want to beat you."

"Is it that much more dangerous to fly aggressive? In 1992 I had twelve friends killed. It was like someone was dying every other weekend. And it was bad. People would ask me about it. I had a good buddy of mine who was killed right near my house, at Eloy airport, that year practicing. And people will go, 'Well you're better than they are.' And I say, 'No, you know what, in this sport you live and you learn or you die and you don't.' And there's plenty of times I probably should have died and I came out and I was just lucky enough and I just missed it."

The Chinese were waiting. Kirby strapped on his chute and climbed into his plane. He pushed forward the small lever that primed the engine and then hit the ignition, sending the prop spinning as the engine kicked to life. Kirby taxied his plane to the end of the runway and quickly checked the controls, putting the stick around all four corners to make sure there were no jams. He ran the engine up, moved the propeller control back and forth. The engine surged as he adjusted the blades. He stretched his head back and forth a half-dozen times to loosen up his neck muscles, which would contract under the high-g loads. Then he taxied into position, hit the power, and rolled down the runway and up into the sky.

The flight to the hole took one minute. As Kirby raced in

he could see the thousands of faces below. He watched as a pilot zipped into the hole ahead of him, rolling the plane as he went. Okay, so that trick was out. Kirby shot up to the mouth of the hole, nearing 150 miles an hour. He leveled the plane off and steadied himself against the turbulence. Not as bad as he expected. He was in the hole in a second and, moments later, as he shot out the other end he yanked back hard on the stick and pulled up into a loop. Up and over the hole he arced, and then shot back right into the mouth of the damn thing. A loop! He could almost hear the glee of the Chinese as he screamed past again and pulled hard to get back into the hole, bouncing around a bit. As he pulled up again, a big California grin worked across Kirby's face. "Let them top that," he was thinking. "Let Jurgis fucking top that." But what was lurking in the back of Kirby's mind as he pulled away on that second loop was this: he had heard they might be invited back next year to fly under a 1,000-year-old bridge with twenty-three feet of water clearance. Could he loop that?

Kirby was going about 200 miles an hour when he hit the water. If you talked to the people who saw it they explained how the wings had come off first, turning the plane into a bullet, how the left wing had just barely touched the river and then the whole collection—plane, Kirby, water—had just become a blur of junk. It was as if you had taken reality and put it into a blender. There was just this kind of stew in front of your eyes. It was brown like the water, blue and white in places, like Kirby's plane. Right on the other side of the bridge, just opposite where Kirby had flown under. Nobody could see the pink that must be Kirby's body, but they figured that might be some kind of blessing. Maybe it was just over, over in a hurry for him. And, gosh, it *was* fast. Of course Kirby had always liked it like that: blazing. But this really was so speedy, it was so just gunshot-quick. That was what really stayed with people afterward, this parable of how our world can collide with our hopes and how it can do it so fast we don't have time to shout, or say a prayer, or say good-bye.

The amazing thing, and this really was amazing, was that Kirby was okay. The Chinese raced out to the plane, his fellow pilots raced out, all of them in a furious sprint-swim to the mess lying out there on the water. Blood streaming down his face, Kirby teetered out of the crumpled plane. The Chinese helped him onto a boat.

When he got home, Kirby found that his wife had had the engine taken off his plane. No more flying. But two months later he was back in the sky. Airshow season lingered ahead. It was a team selection year for the United States. He needed the practice. He needed the flying. Let Jurgis fucking top that.

It is still dark.

I t is still dark. New York City is caught in a five A.M. half-sleep, stumbling quietly home after a forgettable night. In the back of a taxi, I am headed to the airport and Florida for aerobatics training. I am browsing the latest issue of *Sport Aerobatics* magazine in the strobing city lights as we speed up Third Avenue, tunnel-bound. Omens, I must remind myself, are to be avoided.

On December 14, 2000, about 0950 Eastern Standard Time, a Christen Pitts S-2B, N260DB, registered to and operated by a private individual as a Title 14 CFR Part 91 personal flight, crashed in the Everglades, near Weston, Florida. Visual meteorological conditions prevailed, and no flight plan was filed. The aircraft incurred substantial damage, and the private-rated pilot and one pilot-rated passenger were fatally injured. The flight originated from Hollywood North Perry Airport, Hollywood, Florida, about 0900.

According to a Federal Aviation Administration (FAA) contract tower controller at the Hollywood North Perry Airport, at 0950 he received a radio communications transmission saying, "Mayday mayday mayday. Pitts 260DB in an unrecoverable flat spin at 3,500 feet." In addition, a detective with the Broward County Sheriff's Office stated that a sheriff's office dispatcher received a cell telephone call from a motorist traveling along Interstate 75 (Alligator Alley) about 0953, stating that he/she had just observed an airplane crash into the Everglades, in the vicinity of the rest stop at mile marker 35. The airplane was discovered in a wooded marshy area of the Everglades, slightly west of the rest stop, in about 3 feet of water. The aircraft had incurred substantial damage, and the pilot and passenger were found outside the aircraft, and had both sustained fatal injuries.

December fourteenth is my birthday. This is exactly the sort of thing it does not serve to stare at for too long. Two grown men, strapped inside a small airplane, spinning uncontrollably at the ground on my birthday, spinning slowly enough that they had time not only to know their fate, but to bespeak their doom to anyone who might be listening. Imagine the strange, violent scene. All the unnerving small details. That radio call? The nervous thumb mashed hard onto the transmit button. Why not use the time to bail out of the plane? Why talk? At the crash site, the police found the pilot cranked halfway out of the cockpit, half-snapped by the impact as he tried to bail out too low; his passenger was several hundred feet away with a partially inflated chute. Also too late for salvation. The pilot was no amateur. He was an airline captain and president of his local aerobatic club.

Engineers insist that any spin, with the proper shuffling of our hands and feet, is recoverable. Yet here was a pilot who had more aerobatic time than I, who walked up to the wall that sits on the final edge of flight and spun right through the damn thing. If he could speak to me, I find myself wondering, if we gave him an extra few seconds to piss away on useless radio chatter, what would he say? "Leave the peace and happiness of this New York City spring morning, pack your things and go strap into an airplane in which you can kill yourself with a misplaced thought or an overlooked item on your preflight inspection. Leave. Go fly." Did he die on my birthday to send that message?

The risk of the sport lingers in my brain somewhere. It is like a name you cannot quite recall. But it eludes me in the end, it never moves off the tip of my tongue. Sometimes I feel hints. Quick moments when the plane squirts off in an unexpected direction, or I find myself moving faster or closer to the ground than I planned. Then the thing comes so hard it is the only truth. My adrenaline-shot legs cramp, my heart rockets. I will be brought to understand later, after hours of flying, that this instinct is the very thing that makes it safe to stay in the cockpit. But I wonder if I will have a moment when I will go beyond it, to a quieter place that comes with the certainty of knowing what is about to happen. I had a short glimpse of it, I suppose, that lovely summer day over the ocean when I started a pull too low and nearly spread myself out onto the water. It was nothing more than luck and a habit of setting my altimeter 200 feet low before takeoff that saved me. But in the end I had only a small taste, a sample of the theory. It was a kind of astonishment that I could mistake myself to death, a near amazement that my faith was unjustified.

This was why you couldn't deny the creeping itch of those omens. Even the best pilots, the Kirbys, felt it. "After that, I left the plane in the hangar for a couple of weeks," pilots will sometimes say to one another. It is a code, shorthand for the lapses. We have seen behind the curtain. It is an accident; it takes us a little time to recover ourselves. In the hard early days of my training, these glances even hurt sometimes. They were as much a fact of the flying as aerodynamics. More than a panicky sense of unease, it was something other than that adrenaline rush. Psychologists like to make a distinction between terror and fear. Terror is the fast, bolting chemical reaction. Fear is a slower burn. Fear was like a cocktail of regret that offered me a taste of a world forsaken. I could feel the plane spinning, see the earth and sky flapping incoherently in front of my eyes. And "Shit, shit, shit!" is all I hear in my head. It is night, I am lying awake, staring at the ceiling. My reaction is just as I would like: my left hand chops the power, my right jams the stick to the inside of the spin to remove the flatness, and my foot mashes on the rudder on the opposite side of the turn. After a few rotations the spin turns into a dive. With a four-g pull up, I am away and safe. Why is my heart beating?

Do you know Botticelli's painting of Giuliano de Medici? The one where the scion stares blithely out of the canvas as a medieval Florentine sky snakes out over his shoulder. A small brown bird nestles at the edge of the frame, a painterly symbol that the already-dead Giuliano (knifed while attending high mass a year before this portrait was made) has gone to heaven. In the center of the canvas Giuliano has the marble confidence of a man born to rule. His eyes have the heat, the energy you see in kids. His chest is full, a balloon under that red jerkin, like he's been caught mid-breath. But what makes this 500-year-old painting kick at your heart, what makes you swallow when you look deep into it, is the hint that creeps up the side of his face. It is hurt as fresh as a punch. You might almost mistake it for a grin, this tiny twitch. But it is more. He is looking back from immortality. Helplessly.

How do you train someone to operate in an environment that is both terrifying and fantastic? It is not simply about acquiring skills, because the skills can desert you in moments of urgency. Real training is about learning faith. In the fifteenth century biblical scholars got into a very heated debate about the Old Testament story of Abraham at the moment God asks him to sacrifice his son as a proof of loyalty. Why do we celebrate Abraham for complying, scholars argued with one another? He was so faithful at that point, had climbed so many rungs of the ladder toward God, that his obedience was instinctive. We celebrate Abraham, the rabbis explained, because when God asks you to sacrifice your only son you are suddenly stripped of every piece of your faith, you are sent back to the lowest rung on the ladder. The moment is both terryfing and fantastic. It is like asking you to sacrifice your own life. And what you choose to do next, on that bottom rung of the ladder, is the sign of your true faith.

Often in aerobatics you will face situations that you have never seen before. Once you pass beyond a certain level of difficulty, formal training in how to push and pull the plane becomes irrelevant. All you have is instinct. What matters most is your confidence. In the flying world, among truly elite pilots, test pilots say, aerobatics flyers are regarded not as suicidal but as disciplined. They are seen as practitioners of a more extreme kind of faith that all pilots share, a faith that can produce otherworldly beauty. It is so hard to accomplish an epiphany. To the average pilot one may come every few hundred hours, on a quiet night, say, when the city lights are passing silently underneath and the radios are muted and the sky is tranquil. This is an incredible and perfect moment. The lure of aerobatics is that you can re-create this epiphany much more often. It is the reward, the fantastic reward, for the risk. It is, in some of our minds, an early glimpse of heaven. And this explains why it is such a wonderful auto-da-fé, such a perfect act of faith.

The great aerobatics teachers fall into two categories, the crazy and the deliberate. For several years I was the student of an aging aerobatic pilot I will simply call Charlie. "There are old pilots and bold pilots," a flying saw goes, "but no old, bold pilots." Except Charlie. He was a seventy-year-old man with the adrenaline needs of a fourteen-year-old and the judgment of a toddler. Preflight checks consisted of starting the airplane. Postflight debriefings took the form of stories that ended with the phrase "that was back when I was drinking" and an irreverent flick of his Zippo lighter in the gas-filled hangar. Many of Charlie's fables featured a character he called "the Monk," an actual member of a holy order who shared Charlie's faith in the limitless miracles of mixed airplanes and alcohol. Simple plot lines, these stories. Charlie and the Monk get loaded, climb into a plane (the Monk gingerly socking his rough cassock under the seat belts), and then fly inverted over some charitable event dropping things on it in accordance with an opaque sense of symbolism: golf balls on a Special Olympics race, for instance. Watermelons on a church bake sale.

Charlie's particular gift came from a fingertip feel of how to handle the plane at speeds just above a stall. Traveling at fifty or sixty miles an hour he could manage aerobatics that usually required twice the speed. From him I learned how to handle the low-energy twists and turns that the sport often demands, how to get the airplane to move precisely with just a wisp of wind passing over the wings. "Easy," Charlie would say through the intercom as we teetered along at treetop height and rolled the plane. *Easy.* It was his word for relax, for not doing the thing you most wanted to do, which was to move the plane fast and hard. Maybe it was his word for an old man's faith. "And then this." He would dance the plane around a roll in the same way you might shrug your shoulders, all muscles and reflex. The trick, as much as there was one, was in cheating the nose down just a bit at every opportunity. These little knits in the air picked up one, two miles an hour at a time. But like plucking pennies from a wish pond, it was possible eventually to accumulate enough money for a meal.

Don't think this required only patience. It demanded too a masseuse's feel for the airplane. I never managed it in Charlie's Pitts. But once, over Newark late at night in a Piper with ice creeping up while I was stuck in an air-traffic hold, I felt Charlie. The wings moved ponderously through the turn, heavy with frost and ice. "Easy," I thought as I rolled into a gentle, instrument-only 180-degree turn deep inside a cloud. But Charlie's flying was too dangerous to take me where I hungered to go now. Serious competition required a discipline he no longer possessed. I had seen that Zippo lighter once too often.

Top pilots devour guidance. David Martin, an American genius in everything from a Piper Cub to an F-16, set his eyes on the World competition in 1992 and began eating a week's worth of Sergei's instruction every month, sometimes more. There's nothing weak here. Aerobatics is, like our lives, a solitary sport at the end. And there is a purity there. But mastery is beyond the loner's heart; form demands help. It demands good eyes on the ground and reliable advice. The tiniest mistake can become an ingrained habit that takes years to repair. Small errors setting lines at 250 miles an hour are quickly spelled out in the sky. So I began to devour help too. In the end, I would seek it from three men. Sergei Boriak pushed me to throw the plane violently through the sky, and then a concrete-hard Vietnam vet named Phil Knight brought me a sense of how to carve a sculpture of beauty and grace, something that would score well with judges. But first I had to learn to fly the plane. For that job I selected Alan Bush, a U.S. Airways captain who happened to be America's first aerobatics prodigy.

If you spotted Alan at work, wandering the Philadelphia air terminal, ducking smoothly into a crew-only room for instance, you'd most likely mistake him for another forget-table flying pretty boy, anonymous until a jet engine quits or you have to divert to another airport. Bush looks like five feet nine inches of central-casting airline pilot. He has the airline haircut, that blow-dried helmet with the even, rounded hair-line that stops midway between a captain's hat and collar. His skin is coated with the satin tan of a low-handicap golfer. The looks deceive. Before he was twenty-one, Bush was humping night cargo from Haiti to Florida in busted-up WWII trans-ports, coaxing the old brutes through tropical thunderdawns and onto beat-up dirt runways. He left that gig to become the youngest airline captain in U.S. history.

In 1976, aged eighteen, Alan just missed qualifying for the U.S. National Team when he zeroed a figure on his final flight. It was a silly mistake, and the forty-year-old guys who did make the team liked him so much that they dragged him along to Moscow for the competition. *Be the mechanic*, they said. Alan drove the team truck into Russia from Germany. Each country was allowed a warm-up flight before competi-tion began, a chance for a noncompeting pilot to work through the skies to get a sense of the wind and the lay of the box. The U.S. team pulled Alan out of his truck and sent him up as their warm-up. The Soviet teams stopped their chatter to watch. "Jeesus," they said to one another as Bush flew. "This is their *mechanic*?"

The mechanic has an extraordinary gift for flight. These days he trains idly, if at all, but routinely notches finishes among the top dozen pilots in the United States. His flying is mysterious in its emotional charm. On the ground he is all frat boy. In the air, all Nijinsky. Once, on a hot summer day, I saw him lazily draw his plane earthward in a flat spin—the figure that killed those two men in Florida—from several thousand feet. The plane looked like a red-and-white pinwheel against the sky. Inside, Alan was being thrown hard against the straps, but from the ground the effect was nothing short of deliberate magnificence. Over and over again the plane snapped around, reflecting sun off the canopy as it settled. The propeller emitted a weak, angry whine as the plane fell through the cloudless sky, like a motorcycle revving. At just the moment when this reverie was likely to become dangerous, perhaps 300 feet, he popped the plane free and flew off on exactly the same heading he had begun with. A masterstroke.

Alan and I started with a simple problem: teaching me to land my plane. Easily the most noticeable difference between my Extra and the other planes I'd flown had nothing to do with aerobatics: the Extra has its third wheel affixed under the tail instead of under the nose. In the early days of flight tail-wheel design was the only choice for airplanes: by keeping the nose up, a tail-wheel helped put the plane in a flying attitude, it put the wings at an angle where the airflow provided the most lift, and it made it possible to swing bigger propellers around the nose. But by the late 1940s manufacturers began moving the third wheel from tail to the nose to add stability. The new configuration also gave pilots better visibility on the ground when taxiing and more control in the moments just before the gear touched the ground. But for some reason, most aerobatic planes have continued to hold on to the old design. Partly it's aerodynamic—the planes all carry oversized props—but it's also the ethos of the sport. The rakish planes that, even sitting still, look ready to fly.

But since the tail wheel on aerobatic planes is located *behind* the plane's center of gravity, it tends to act like a pivot. A strong gust on landing can kick a mishandled tail-wheel plane right off the runway or into a ground-loop, in which the plane begins turning so quickly on the ground that it dips a wing and catches the turf, sometimes flipping over on its back. This makes the plane terribly unstable on the ground. At the NASA test-pilots school, a tail-wheel Pitts, famously tough to land and taxi, is the only plane the students aren't allowed to fly by themselves. And while landing a tail-wheel plane, the nose is raised so high that it's nearly impossible to see anything ahead of your propeller. You are landing so blindly that a little side-drift can be impossible to detect until you touch down half on, half off the runway and spin out to the side, turning your $200,000 plane into slag. Even taxiing the plane is done blindly behind the high nose. Several years ago at the U.S. Nationals, two experienced tail-wheel pilots taxied head-on into each other in front of a stand full of awestruck, screaming judges.

Alan and I began landing practice on a wide runway at St. Augustine and slowly moved over to a narrower, shorter track. There are no flaps or spoilers on the Extra, devices that most planes use to create extra drag when landing. Slowing the Extra down for landing meant using an extreme sideslip on final approach, bringing the plane down to the runway cock-eyed, then kicking out straight at the last moment. It's an unnerving sight the first few times. Instead of lining up with the center line and driving to the runway, the kind of approach you're used to from jetliner flight, aerobatic pilots chop the power off at about 900 feet and then glide in a circle toward the runway, jam in the rudder to skew the plane. The simplest way to lose airspeed—lifting the nose—works to a certain extent, but you can't pull the nose too high or the plane will stop flying altogether.

I suffered, at first. It was like being back in initial flight training. I had the usual problem of transitioning pilots, a tendency to overcontrol the plane during the rollout, stabbing at the brakes instead of applying gentle hints of pressure. But after a few hours of tail-wheel time, I was pretty sure I could put the plane down on almost any runway and haul it to a stop in less than 1,000 feet.

What was harder to get used to was the responsiveness of the plane. Whatever I thought, I could do. The plane tore through the air. It twisted faster than I could keep track of. I would pull into a vertical line, start what was supposed to be a single roll, and end up around nearly twice before I could decode the magic. I had had dreams about flying this way. The actual plane was better.

There were nightmares too. I was on final approach one day with Alan in the front seat. We were at about 500 feet and I moved the stick slightly more abruptly than I intended. Perhaps an inch, the kind of thing you might do as you bend over to adjust a map or the volume on your radio. Suddenly we were up on a wing. I stabbed the stick back to level flight. And the plane came in easily to land. I was too distracted to pay much attention to the landing, so naturally it was perfect. But the speed of that upset was heartwrenching. It put me in mind of the last ominous moments of those Pitts pilots, a sense that the plane had gone into a dark and mysterious corner of the flight envelope. In a quarter-second we had shot from quiet control to something very near an accident. I was sure I wasn't going to make that mistake on the stick again, but I was shaken by how quickly the plane moved off line, how quickly it could turn me into a passenger. The very thing that made it a perfect aerobatic mount also made it a potential killer.

Alan and I went for lunch after I landed. We ate in silence. I wrapped my hand around a frosted glass of lemonade and then pressed my cold fingers to my temples. I snapped my head around a couple of times, loosening my neck. In as much as Alan had a philosophy of flight it was this: fly the plane. It was too easy to become a passenger, to let the Extra slip into chaos. "You doin' okay?" he asked. "Yeah," I said. He looked out the window for a little while. We walked back to the plane together. "Look," he said, "why don't you take it up for a little while by yourself." He reached in front and pulled his chute out, fastened up the belts there so they were out of the way. "Get comfortable. Do something amazing." I strapped in and started the plane, looking out over the prop without the familiar sight of Alan's head. I taxied out, quickly ran the preflight checks, and took position on the runway. Cleared to takeoff, I gunned the throttle and pushed in a little right rudder to keep the plane tracking down the center-line. I could feel my nervous foot bouncing a bit against the rudder.

I pulled up hard away from the traffic pattern, trying to scare the shakes out of my foot, trying to leach the quiver from my soul. The sky opened in front of me. I checked that my belts were tight and slammed the plane inverted as hard as I could and pointed myself out to the practice area. It was five minutes distant. I flew upside down the whole way.

*Just to be around
Leo Loudenslager was
something else.*

J ust to be around Leo Loudenslager was something else. His faith was strong. His greatness was bloody and painful. It sounded like this: "I was scared. The plane was very unstable in some maneuvers and I was flying so hard and pulling so many negative g's that the broken blood vessels in my eyes made them look like a rabbit's. I thought I was dying." Or this: "It used to be I'd be pushing the nose under into a maneuver needing high negative g's and I'd hear myself beginning to whimper from the pain. I'd keep telling myself I'd do just one more maneuver and then I'd come down. Some days I'd keep saying that through a hundred and fifty maneuvers." His intensity was like a cold. It gave him the shakes, a short temper, a fever to win. It was contagious. And just to be within five feet of Leo was enough to get you sick too. If you were a fellow aerobatic pilot, if you were good enough to inhabit that thin air of world-class Unlimited jocks, if you had faith too, then getting near Leo Loudenslager was, oh God.

Say it was 1974 and Leo was flying his Laser, the prototype of the plane that would eventually end up in the Smithsonian with his name next to it. When he took off everything on the ground would just stop. The long-hairs at a contest in their Beetles, the crop-dusters who'd come out to see what they could do against the airline boys, every one of them would just freeze and look up for as long as it took. There went Leo again, reworking every law of physics about fifty feet off the ground. He was operating beyond physics really, he was living after gravity. You could hear the plane groaning with the effort, the prop screaming in tailslides as it fought against the backward-running air current. Watching Leo was like watching a suicide, some of his fellow competitors said. It was all too fast, too low, too dangerous. Leo on the ground was sometimes funny. He joked, made goofy expressions with his handsome face, wore silly shirts. But Leo in the air was American summer made perfect. For the pilots who admired him, he was every good day you had in your whole life stuffed into a four-minute sequence. Leo was beyond perfect, he was beautiful.

The year 1974 may seem like a strange place to begin a history of aerobatics. Why not start off with Nesterov, the Russian who flew the first loop in Kiev in 1913? Or Jimmy Doolittle cranking around the first *outside* loop in 1931, lighting up his Army Air Corps commander?

"How dare you do that to a U.S. government airplane!"

"How could I not?" Doolittle, one of the first high priests, snaps back. But beginning there would be like starting a history of art with pictures of cave drawings. They are important, sure. But Caravaggio! Leonardo! Picasso! There's the meat. So Loudenslager.

Leo insisted it was all just work. That was part of the charm, the modesty of a seven-time U.S. national champion insisting he simply worked harder than everybody else. He'd knock his uneven blond hair back, brush at his long sideburns, and explain it was all just the practice, the thousands of hours in the air. He did work harder than anyone, of course. His whole life was tuned around the sport. "Do you have any hobbies," a reporter once asked him, writing one of the many profiles that would edge Leo beyond the narrow world of aerobatics and closer to wider triumph. "Uh, skiing," he stammered after a pause. "Well, sometimes I ski. But there isn't much room for anything but aerobatics." He moved his family three times, to three states, to find a patch of open grass where he could fly aerobatics without triggering a barrage of "that maniac!" calls to the FAA. And even then the calls came and the visits from friends and the quiet words delivered in still moments: *Leo, you are flying too dangerously. You have a family.*

As Leo saw it, the sport had to own your mind, it had to possess your heart. There were doubts, sure. But he had a rigorous and unshakable kind of faith, a crusader's faith, which sees martyrdom as a process not a moment. So his revolution began in his brain, with his unquestioned confidence. Maybe there was something wrong there? Maybe there was something broken in his mind? When he was eight, playing Little League ball for the very first time, he decided he was going to hit a home run in his first at bat. He stood there for three strikes, amazed as the pitches floated past. He didn't even get the bat off his shoulder. When he was called out, Leo began crying so uncontrollably that the coaches rushed to see where he was hurt. The ball had come nowhere near him. He had found something that hurt more than physical pain. Losing fired a pain that was awful, far worse than anything aerobatics could cause. It was better to whimper in the cockpit than to stare, late at night, out your window at a life that doesn't match up to what you want from yourself. Losing meant your faith was misplaced. "I'm not fearless, but I try to translate my fear into respect for the plane and the conditions," he said. And into victory. "I accept the fact that I may die in that airplane."

So Leo began his revolution inside his own head, developing a willful focus and unshakable certainty about his plane. This was long before the days of men like Patrick Paris, the Frenchman who won the World Aerobatic Championship in 1998 after an Odyssean, decade-long journey of trying to shake the bads from his flying. Though indisputably one of the best European pilots since the War, he had finished fourth twice and second twice before finally winning the World Championship. "I realized from year to year that something was wrong in my preparation. Even if I tried psychology, yoga and so on. It was not enough," Paris once said of his quest to become a World Aerobatic Champion. So in 1997 he began literally reformatting his brain using neurolinguistic programming, changing the meaning of words like *win* and *fear*. "By making all of these approaches of mental preparation," he said later, "I realized that I finally had the feeling I was now ready to win and that I wanted strongly to win. I am happy that it took me a long time to become World Champion because I learned a lot about me and others. It was, in fact, like an intricate path you find in Oriental philosophy."

Leo's journey was strictly occidental, all Western hurry and bluster. He needed no programming. The gold-rush Californian in him just sprinted for what he wanted, to win, and excluded everything else. "First," he explained to new pilots, "you must realize that it's going to take up a great deal of time and money. Quite often my advice to an aspiring pilot is to get a great job. Ask yourself first where is the time and money coming from? Aerobatics doesn't pay for itself, you must support it." This was classic Leo. He could get it to pay, if he wanted. He could spend every weekend doing airshows, plastering logos on the sides of his fire-engine-red plane. The networks came to him and offered to pay if he'd fly on TV. Sometimes he did, but Leo was after something more pure, flights whose ends were simply perfection and then victory. "Back when I was a flight instructor," Leo once recalled, "I came to the conclusion that talent is basically a cheap commodity. There is a lot of talent around and a lot of people have the talent to fly and fly very well, to be an aerobatic pilot and to win. But the point is that talent is nothing without a tremendous amount of work. There is no easy way to success. Aerobatics is no different than any other endeavor in life. Without the work it just doesn't come."

Leo's practices were brutal. Four, five times a day he would fly in the hottest heat he could find. He wanted the extra drain of the sweat. It is easier to black out when you are hot, harder to control your body in the plane. And every flight had to be perfect or Leo was furious. It was Little League baseball all over again. He pushed himself beyond the limits of the rational. He never made a mistake twice. From the outside, it was like watching a man make himself from clay. "He would go up and you would tell him there was a problem and he would fix it right away," says Clint McHenry, a champion pilot himself and Leo's nearest competitor. "You would never see it again. He could mold himself into any kind of pilot he wanted to be." Leo wanted to reduce, as much as possible, the distinction between pilot and airplane. "This is a contest *between* pilot and airplane," he said of world-class aerobatics. He didn't see it as a battle against other pilots, but as a struggle to get his machine to do what he wanted. A battle with himself.

Loudenslager was born in Columbus, Ohio, and stayed through high school, before joining the Air Force as a jet mechanic. In the Air Force he managed to get a few aerobatic flights in a T-34 trainer, but he had almost no aerobatic time in his logbook when he left the Air Force and joined American Airlines as a pilot, in 1966, for the paycheck. He knew early on that the kind of flying he wanted to do couldn't be done in the planes available, so as soon as he became involved with aerobatics, he began building his own. He knew he wanted a monoplane, since the one-wing design was the dominant choice for international competition. At a contest, he saw an American-designed monoplane called the Stevens Acro that belonged to Margaret Ritchie, one of the best women pilots in the United States. He had to have one, even after Ritchie was killed in a training accident flying the prototype. He had never built a plane before. "I committed myself to build one out of blind faith and an intuition that it was the right thing to do," he said later.

The plane had some design flaws, potentially lethal. It suffered from "stick-snatch," an aerodynamic fault that caused the stick to shoot out of the pilot's hand in certain maneuvers. It was a terrifying quirk, making already uncontrollable maneuvers unpredictable. Leo described the fear: "More than once I'd push forward for an outside snap and my teeth would be chattering, my knees would be shaking and it would go WHAP! I always came through, but I sure didn't feel very good about it." Another design problem emerged when Loudenslager started pushing the plane into hard negative g's. As the forces built up, the stick became harder and harder to push. Ten, twenty, fifty pounds of push to get around a loop. Leo's arm strength couldn't keep up with the demands of the plane he had built.

But by 1972, just a year into competition, he was finishing among the top five in the U.S. Nationals. Even in his first few months of flying, his peers saw something in the way he flew. No one could name it yet, but Leo just looked different in the air. He was taking a language they all took for granted and remaking it. From his very first flight. In 1975 he was National Champion. And again in 1976, 1977, and 1978, a record four in a row. In 1978 he nearly won the World Championship before an unintentional rules violation on his last flight. Some said he was screwed by the Soviet-rigged jury.

Loudenslager was figuring out how to win—and, in the process, remaking the way pilots flew. He began with that plane, the Laser, constantly refining it. He was maniacal about getting weight off to enhance performance, finally stripping it down to 842 pounds (A flight-school Cessna weighs about 1,800 pounds) by doing everything from drilling holes in his canopy mount to sanding away extra metal from the engine. He

once engaged a chemist in a long discussion about the possibility of using acid to etch away the insides of the steel tubes of his
airframe to save a few ounces.

What he did on the plane was a preview of what he did in
the air. Before Leo, aerobatics still had a graceful pace. It was
slower, less aggressive flight. Leo wanted it to be different.
Now. In his air-show performances, he'd pull to vertical and do
a three-quarter vertical snap roll . . . on takeoff! Standing still in
the air, he'd kick the plate over and fly away. "I got on him. I
said I can't believe what you are doing," Clint McHenry, a fellow competitor, said. "If his engine failed he's dead." But nothing could stop him. In competition Leo chose the chance to
win over everything: his health, his plane, at times his life. In
1978, competing at the World Championships in Czechoslovakia he ended up too low on a figure and in a fraction of a second
had to decide between staying safe and winning. "Two thoughts
shot through my mind," he recalled. He was low, too low, on a
vertical downline and needed to begin an altitude-consuming
snap roll. He was pointing straight down—there is no faster
route to the ground. "One: if you're going to have a chance at
this contest you've got to go for it, and two: can you get away
with this without killing yourself? Well, I thought, 'Goodbye to
Suzy and the kids.' I knew I didn't have time to rethink. I did it.
I was shaken by it and really went down through the floor of
the box, but I went on. The next pilot came even closer to
killing himself."

And the other pilots had to follow him. One day in 1904,
Georges Braque visited Pablo Picasso in his Paris studio and
saw *Les Demoiselles d'Avignon*, Picasso's revolutionary cubist

painting. Braque was nauseated. "It is like you are trying to make us eat rope and drink paraffin," he complained. The two men split up after a shouting match. Three months later Braque was producing his own cubist masterpieces. You couldn't fight the truth. Even if it tasted like rope or gas, even if it made you whimper when you flew it.

Loudenslager began keeping obsessive notes of his flying. He carried a little lined notebook with him everywhere, listing out each figure and the problems he had flying it. In those days, just *finishing* an unknown sequence—in which the pilot is given a list of figures to fly and no time to practice—without zeroing a figure could win a competition. But by consulting his little book before each unknown flight, by memorizing what he had to do and where, Loudenslager was able to make his unknown flights look as smooth and sharp as if he had been practicing them for weeks. He used every practice session as a chance to work toward mastery of a maneuver. "Perfection," he would say, "is impossible." So four or five times a day, Loudenslager would climb into his plane and take off to polish the way he flew, like some already flawless gem. He never just got into the plane and took off. He flew as if he were in a trance.

In 1980 Leo Loudenslager won the World Championship with a series of violently perfect flights. There is a picture from that last competition night of Leo and Betty Stewart, an American who won the women's World title, standing with their medals hanging around their necks. Leo has the impish grin of the victorious revolutionary. It is the smirk Castro wears in the photo of him and Che playing golf at a Havana country club shortly after La Victoria Gloriosa. Leo's unruly blond hair is lopped over in a feeble effort at a part and his stick-thin arms jut from his flight suit. He looks breakable as crystal. The light reflects from the four medals—one for each flight in competition—so that they look almost white. And though the photo is black and white, Leo seems to have a nearly golden glow. He looks immortal.

How Leo died was this. For years, people said he would die in a plane. Frankly, there were a number of times it looked like a sure bet, times when people watching Leo from the ground would turn their heads away because of what they knew they were about to see next. But Leo always flew off unhurt. Leo got killed on his motorcycle. This was incredible to the pilots who knew him. For a man who took so many risks in the air, who danced so close to the edge, to die on a bike seemed somehow unjust. After all this, after years and years, he gets hit by a car? "Cleaned off a motorcycle," in the awful phrase of a friend of his.

The car was stalled. Something was wrong, it was just parked in the road, jammed into the New Jersey night like an overfilled glass on a table ledge, an object filled with the potential energy of disaster. Something to be avoided. So, in an instant, the end of Leo. He came up on it from behind, swerved left in an arc to miss it, and smashed head-on into a car moving around the corner. He lingered, a semicomatose haze of a man, for a week. As long as people fly aerobatics they will talk about Leo, the way he was a prophet of what was possible in the air.

"I build a cage around myself, pull into a shell so I can reason things out," Leo once said, struggling to explain the intensity that locked him off from the world, the need that ate at him. Sometimes, at a contest, long after Leo had made it, after he was known as the best ever, a friend would offer him a bed for the night, some company in a strange town. He would refuse. Leo Loudenslager would take out a tarp and put it on the cold ground under his wing and go to sleep quietly alone, in air filled with the smell of oil. "I find that I cannot reason and talk," he said. "So, I value my solitude. That makes me look like I'm aloof. My body might be here, in front of you, but my mind is somewhere else."

But if Leo was the best, the tip of the spear, he was still, for all that, a part of *the tradition*. The aerobatics had come as soon as the planes, of course. We couldn't stop ourselves. No pilots could. And in Europe? With all the anger, all the "after you, Gaston" politesse of an elite class that had perfected the art of killing each other over centuries? What better sport could they have? You could kill yourself! With all your friends watching!! Didn't the Germans have one of their long words for that? Thus *the tradition* began. The competitions were an occasional thing before the world wars, an odd air rally in Paris or Lyon or Metz. But even then it was damn serious. Graf von Hagenburg vs. Frantisek Novak in Zurich in 1911. Von Hagenburg's subtle message: *I will be invading your country in three years. Now let's go fly!* You couldn't ignore the politics of the thing. They were part of the fun, actually.

The competition picked up again between the wars. A dozen or so contestants from around Europe, each with new tricks bearing their names, would arrive in some small town to do impossible things. Downward loops with rolls on each corner, flat spins, slow rolls. What was that, they asked one another? The nicknames for the figures, codged up by European aristocrats, invariably sounded like a page from the Budapest phone book. And still the political undercurrent. Some arrogant young Nazi scoring well on a figure he had perfected "over the line in France." Code for something he'd made up one day while shooting down an Oxford classmate of yours in the Great War. Still, *let's go fly!* Then, during the Cold War, it was West against East. No one seemed to care that the enemies had changed. It had to be someone. You had to beat someone. It was as close to pistols at dawn as you could get. The countries poured money in. European pilots became heroes. In France, they named schools for them. In the Soviet Union they appeared in newsreels, models of the new order.

And in America? Speed, my friend, speed. Sure the tricks were nice, but what we wanted here was just fast. So the aerobatics got a slow start, we had no heroes. Air races were the American sport. Coast-to-coast sprints or L.A. to Hawaii or, what the hell, even around a bunch of pylons in downtown Cleveland. (At least until the year, uh, those four planes tumbled out of control and killed a dozen spectators and just missed the schoolyard. The races were moved to the desert, where only the pilots died now. Much better, the sponsors said.) That was America, a country in a hurry. Of course it might be worthwhile to go over to Europe just to see what they were up to there with their little sky bullets. Show the flag, you know. Kick a little European butt. In 1960 a group of European pilots organized the first World Aerobatic Competition in Czechoslovakia. So Frank Price, from west Texas, decided he had better go fly in the damn thing. Remind them who won the war.

Price was a part-time crop-duster who performed at air shows to grease up an awfully thin dust-bowl income. After a long day pushing pesticides at corn crops, he'd unhook the sprayers and head out to fly at fairgrounds. Ten bucks for a half-hour show. Some weekends he was so busy hop-scotching between work and shows that he didn't have time to unplug the sprayers before he flew. So he'd go up, flying amazing little loops and rolls, blowing leftover DDT across the Texas sky. Shit, he didn't know any better.

The Europeans might have been cranking around in planes designed by the same state design bureaus that built their bombers and fighters, but Price was perfectly happy in his Great Lakes biplane. State of the art 1920s technology. There were about fifteen pilots flying any kind of aerobatics in the United States in those days. Frank Price could whip all of 'em. Was there anything else to say? At their little "contests" in Miami, held whenever the pilots could scrape up enough sponsorship money and local curiosity, they would fly hard, pick up some beers, decide among themselves who had flown best, and give the guy a trophy. If that didn't make Frank Price the best damn pilot in the world, then what the hell did?

One day, toward the end of dusting season, Price fired up

the Great Lakes, loaded Mrs. Celesta Price in the front seat, and flew to Dallas. He taxied up to the Pan Am hanger. Could you boys pull my plane apart, put it in crates, and get it to England for the Lockheed Trophy competition? No. Not enough time. Frank Price flew home again. Thinking the whole way. So he had missed that limited contest. What else was out there? "Well, why don't I go to this world competition? Why don't I go to Czechoslovakia?" Price asked his Celesta that night, as if it were the most natural thing in the world. And Celesta, a prototype for good aerobatic spouses everywhere, a woman who had just flown to Dallas and back with her husband in an open-cockpit biplane, asked without a hint of irony: "Well, why don't you?"

So in the late spring of 1960, Frank Price threw some clothes in a canvas parachute bag (*Should he take the overalls? The Stetson?*) and flew to Idlewild field in Queens, New York, destination Europe. Mission: preserve American honor. He popped the wings off, crated up the engine, and sent the whole mess over to Munich on Pan Am. In Germany he rustled up an old Messerschmitt pilot who was wandering around the airport— what a hoot they'd get out of that in Texas!—and the two old boys bolted that damn plane back together. From Munich, Price flew to Vienna, then on to Linz, a west Texas farm boy finding his way using road maps. He flew down the Danube. He passed over the Iron Curtain. The wind felt colder in the cockpit. In Bratislava, he landed on a big military airfield. It was decorated with red stars, MiGs, and angry-looking soldiers. For the first time Frank Price felt uneasy.

The Soviets wanted to make a statement. They had dispatched their best pilots. The finest planes. The biggest flags, Frank wondered? The Soviet Union needed heroes. What more perfect hero-machine than aerobatics. Around the U.S.S.R. the government was building an infrastructure of thousands of aero-clubs to screen the most promising young pilots and then send them, like little Olga Korbut or Nadia Comenici or Mikhail Baryshnikov, to the places where their potential could be polished for the glory of the Soviet state. This was the system that picked out Sergei Boriak and Jurgis Kayris and transformed them.

Frank Price didn't need to make much of a statement. He figured the flying would do the talking. He smiled a lot. Told some jokes. They didn't go over so well. Maybe it was the translation? He flew an airshow routine to show his fellow competitors what the Great Lakes could do. No one cared. Some of the pilots did notice that Frank accidentally took off with a bunch of loose gear in his cockpit. They noticed that it started falling out of his plane in the middle of the routine. He tried to act like it was part of the show. Ha-ha. Finally, they all clustered together for an opening ceremony photo, Frank Price grinning gamely, all alone, in front of an American flag. Next to him ten Soviet clones with shaved heads stood in front of the hammer and sickle, grimacing. That night he went to his first international aerobatics party and watched the Soviet hacks trying to dance to the counterrevolutionary stylings of Marty Robbins. *Elll Paaaasooo*, Marty sang. The Soviets shook their hips mechanically, like broken-legged birds. Frank Price drank a beer and watched with eyes that kept getting bigger. Welcome home, pardner, he said to himself.

But this wasn't like home at all. For starters, Frank Price wasn't the hottest damn pilot at the competition. What Price saw going on overhead wasn't anything like what he was used to. Instead of the freewheeling "drunken farmer" flying that sold crowds in the American flatlands, he was watching incredibly regimented sequences of maneuvers. They were harsh, unlike anything Frank had ever flown, but he came to see that they were beautiful too. And the planes? The things that they could do flabbergasted him. He seriously worried that no one at home would believe him when he described the flights. He wanted a camera. For instance, at the time, perhaps four American pilots could do a vertical roll, but even then it was a cheat. They'd pull up hard until they were flying straight up, roll as quick as they could, and then push out over the top, trying to get the plane flying again before it gassed off on its back. But the Soviet pilots, flying the new Czech-designed Zlin 226, could pull up, set a vertical line, roll, continue on up, and then push or pull or whatever on top. They could roll twice if they wanted. After one day's flying, a Czech pilot took Price up and showed him the Lomcovak, a maneuver that put the plane into a tumbling spin in the sky. No one in the United States had even thought to try that with a plane, let alone make a competition figure out of it. It was like watching a bunch of damned yo-yos, the way these planes flew. Up, down, up, down. Watching the flat, horizontal American competitions was like watching a Frisbee by comparison.

At the same time that the Czechs were pioneering their vertical rolls and tumbles, a Spanish test pilot named Jose

Aresti was developing a scoring and judging system that brought some uniformity to the sport. He was in Bratislava too, talking to Price and others, a small balding man who had abandoned hopes of becoming *un doctor* to fly biplane fighters in the Spanish Civil War. He still had the patient bearing of a physician, though. He'd wander around the contest, decked out in his little white suit, asking pilots what figures they were planning to fly like a doctor taking a case history. And then Jose Aresti would take out a little piece of paper and a pencil and draw a stick figure of the flight as they told him about it. It was like sheet music for flying, a written language for aerobatics. Before Aresti there were dozens of ways to record a flight, everything from free-hand sketches that showed the planes moving like ribbons in the sky to lists that spelled out sequences like a shopping list: "ROLL." "CLIMB." "SPIN." Aresti was obsessed with standardizing the language. He was a good pilot himself, but this obsession with the written language of flight was beyond that. It was almost unbalanced. "It's my vision that somebody can get in an airplane and do anything in the world they want to do in an airplane, like they can do with music," Aresti would say to rooms full of pilots. They would scuffle their feet. *Is this guy nuts?* "In my book there will be a way to find that figure and assign a coefficient of difficulty and score it." Aresti's book already had 3,000 figures.

"But Señor Aresti," the international pilots would say, "our judges can't even keep track of what our people are doing now. This is not going to work. Too many figures!" Aresti was making figures faster than the pilots could learn them. But he knew the sport would catch up. The planes would get better,

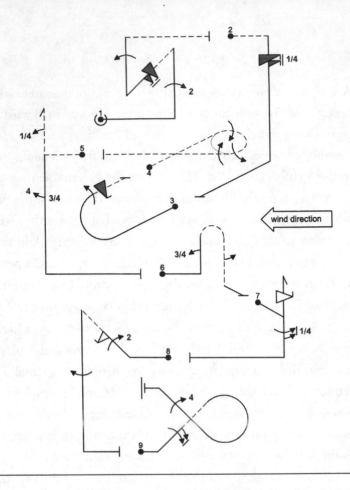

wind direction

the pilots more ambitious. He drew thousands of the little figures. The papers piled waist high in his office. Airline pilots
would stop by to see him as they passed through Madrid. Five
hours later they would still be sitting with Aresti. He wouldn't
let them go. He just wanted to talk about the figures. "You
have to get back to your hotel? Okay, just one more. Look at
this!" *Aresti!* They would say to each other for years, rolling
their eyes. But such a system, such a man with this crazy vision
of an Esperanto for planes, was essential. The pilots had to
agree on what they were flying and how it was going to be

A Typical Unlimited Sequence:
Aresti Notation

The sequence at left is read from the center top of the page.

Begin (1) in level flight into the wind, pull to a vertical upline. Roll the plane 180 degrees, stop hard, then roll another 180 degrees. Wait a beat. Pull onto your back and perform a one-and-a-half outside snap roll. Pull to vertical, roll once, pull onto your back, exit inverted. Two is a one-and-a-quarter rotation inverted spin. Recover into an Immelman turn (3), which is a half-loop, roll on top followed immediately by a one-rotation outside snap. Exit inverted. From inverted, begin (4), a 270-degree turn, rolling the plane three times as you turn, inside, outside, then inside again. Push out inverted (5) into a vertical line. The push may put the maximum negative g's of the sequence onto your plane, about eight. Perform a one-quarter roll on the upline, kick over into a dive, and roll three-quarters of the way around, stopping at each 90 degrees, then pull into level flight. Next (6), pull onto a vertical line, roll three-quarters of the way around and then push over the top, roll 180 degrees on the way down. Seven, pull to vertical, positive snap roll on the way up, hammerhead down, then a one-and-one-quarter roll down. Next (8), pull to 45 degrees up, make a roll with two stops on the upline, then an inside half-snap. Pull down to vertical and roll once. Finally (9), pull to a 45-degree upline, roll one-and-a-half times to inverted, pull through seven-eighths of a loop, and make a four-point roll on the upline. Exit right side up.

————	upright flight
– – – – –	inverted flight
▶	negative snap roll
▷	positive snap roll
↜	roll

---

scored. By 1960, Aresti had divided every possible figure into one of nine categories such as "loops" or "spins." Each was given a number by taking its family number and then adding on another number to indicate any special features. By 2001, there were more than 15,000 coded figures in the aerobatic catalogue. You could say one-dot-six-dot-one, and pilots around the world knew you meant a pull up to a vertical line with a push out to horizontal at the top.

There were hot debates over what exactly the judges were scoring. It wasn't enough just to look at a loop and say it looked round. No, you had to define all kinds of things about the loop. It had to start and stop at the same altitude. It had to be round. Were you scoring the flight path of the plane or the attitude? The speed of the entry or the smoothness? The final system awarded ten points for each figure and then deducted fractions for every deviation from perfection. Drawing on oval instead of a circle in the loop? Minus one point. Come up short of 360 degrees on your roll? Minus a half. The final score was then multiplied by a degree of difficulty, or K factor, for each figure. A roll on a line with one stop halfway through? Eleven points. A spin? Fifteen. And if you take the figure the wrong way, or end up backward or skip it altogether, you get a zero.

The system was good, though it didn't eliminate all the subjectivity. Until the early 1980s it was still possible to screw the best pilot if you were so inclined. Soviet judges would often vote in sync. They had, it emerged, been told who was supposed to win before leaving home. In the 1990s, the sport adopted a computer system that helped eliminate bloc-voting and identified judges who were too far outside the norm. But people just found other ways to play with the system. You had to accept the judging for what it was: the best system for an imperfect task.

Frank Price left Bratislava in 1960 with a twenty-fourth place finish, a photo of himself with some Soviet pilots, and a competition jacket. Given what he had seen there, he was proud not to have finished ass-last. *Fuck this*, the west Texas wanted to say. But something else wanted to hold on to what he had seen, to domesticate it, to Americanize it, to *own* it too. When you see faith stronger than your own you want to embrace it, admire it, not dismiss it. Maybe it was that. Maybe it was that Price had seen some impossible acts in Bratislava and now wanted to collect some of his own. Price became a missionary.

The old country boy headed home via Vienna in formation with a couple of British pilots. The next day he split with them, flew toward Munich, and was forced down into an open Austrian field by lowering clouds and a gas leak. As he sat in the rainy field and waited for reserve fuel to flow into his tank, Frank Price realized he had seen a revolution. His plane was out of date. His ideas were inadequate. And his flying, he was willing to admit to himself, was less than perfect. He would change it all when he got home. Two years later the United States would have its first national championship. Twelve years later it would win its first world contest. Twenty years later Leo Loudenslager would remake the world. Frank couldn't see all that then, of course, though he would be instrumental in making it happen. But he trusted it was real. Trusted it with the same spirit that made him load up and fly halfway around the world in the first place, the same faith that had delivered up this field in the country as the clouds gathered in. He could hear the gas settling into his tanks now. The rain picked up. A young boy and his father came running across the Austrian field to look at the plane, jumping through the mud. They greeted him with a mouthful of unintelligible German. "Water," Price mimed at them. "Water." The boy ran off and brought back a beer. Price sucked it down, started the plane, and flew back up to Munich following a railroad track.

When you saw Frank Price

in the furrows of the

Austrian landschaft . . .

When you saw Frank Price in the fresh furrows of the Austrian *landschaft* thinking over the beauty of what he had seen, you were in the presence of it—the antidote to fear you were looking for all along. This was what the ancient Japanese poets had known, staring terrified at what lingered ahead. They groped for the brush, for beauty. You could see it in that line Neil Williams drew on the grass of that British airfield, or in a glimpse of Leo Loudenslager asleep under his wing at night. You might have spied it in that tumbling mess that was Kirby Chambliss's terrible act of faith in a Chinese river. That old conglomeration of truth and beauty and faith. It was like studying a living Grecian urn, one that contained the answer to Socrates' question of what a virtuous life really looked like.

In his dialogues, Socrates suggested a world where all the questions we faced could be ordered and classified like items in a card catalog. Truth was accessible to anyone who knew the Dewey decimal system. The names—the Crito, the Euthyphro, the Meno—had the unapproachability of old Roman nobility, but in fact each was simply named for Socrates' interlocutors. It was like naming *corridas* for the dead bulls. He had a lethal logic. Lethal even, eventually, to himself. The dialogues were gorgeous to read. There was none of the totalizing systematology of Kant or St. Augustine, though they were beautiful thinkers, too. But there was none of the arrogance of "here is the world explained." Socrates had been too modest even to write them down himself. In one of the dialogues, Menon, a friend of Socrates, engages him in a debate over the nature of knowledge, which is really a debate about virtue. Menon has done well for himself. He is a success, and like many successful people believes that he owes his good fortune to his talents. Intelligence, he explains to Socrates, is a gift of the gods.

Perhaps, says Socrates. But he is not convinced. How, he wonders, would the gods decide who was to receive intelligence? How exactly would they measure it out? Why were some people smart about some things and not others? The objections pile up. So the old master conjures a proof. Send me your slave boy, he told Menon.

The boy ran in and sat at Socrates' side. The old man handed him a small stick and the two of them began tracing lines in the sand floor. Do you know the area of a square? he asked the boy. He did not. Socrates began exploring the geometry of a square, and questioned the boy with the precision of a surgeon. The answers tumbled out, and soon the slave, somewhat bewildered, discovers that he has correctly calculated the area of a square. You see, Socrates explained to Menon, knowledge is inside all of us. It was like a field waiting to be plowed. If the slave boy could become a geometer, who among us was not capable of amazing things?

. . .

One day at the end of my training, I took the plane up, turning out low over the beaches of St. Augustine. I climbed slowly in the humid May air, looking for a hole in the clouds where I could practice. All around me thunderheads were working up into the sky. There was a small slit in the clouds up ahead and, flying knife-edge, I was able to squeeze through and into a bowl of clear air. Though the turbulence inside was rattling me nonstop, it was clear and open enough to let me practice vertical spins and pulls. I ratcheted my belts down at 4,000 feet and pushed over near-vertical into a speed dive, past 200 miles an hour. At 2,000 feet I started my fast flat seven-g pull to level flight. I settled for an instant, shrugged off a twenty-foot turbulent lurch, and cranked hard and fast full back on the stick to an upline. I jerked my left hand off the throttle and slammed it against the prop lever, goosing it past redline as the plane fought for vertical airspeed. As the line trickled out, I pushed two-and-a-half negative g's onto a level topline and then kicked the plane into a one-rotation spin. At 1,500 feet I began to pull to level flight. I settled hard back on the stick, feeling the airflow resistance on the controls as I came through 45 degrees. And then I blacked out.

How long? Five seconds? Ten? Around me the clouds kept up their steady percolation. And my world of pure black remained undisturbed.

I think Socrates' real point to Menon is that knowledge and virtue come from inside us. Even the slave boy has it within him. Truth is locked up in our souls, accessible by each of us without the busy minds of priests, the clammy hands of gods, the selfish demands of kings. The gods don't make some people evil and some good, some smart and some stupid. We all have fields of decency that we can cultivate or not. We all know what is right and just and true. A failure to act in accordance with what we know is no one's fault but our own.

In every life there must be some moments at which this discussion takes place in our souls, where we discover how we are made and what we are made for. These are moments where we decide if we are going to do the right thing or not. I am sure a good argument can be made that no such moments exist, that in fact our whole lives constitute this dialectic. Perhaps some people, like Menon, believe this. But I am among those who believe instances occur that help us understand where we fit. As I imagine them now, they are beautiful, solid things. They seem immortal.

What is extreme flying for me but a kind of dialogue? A conversation with myself about what I am capable of. I am trying to discover in myself something. What: Toughness? Willfulness? Courage? As long as I can remember, I have been setting myself tests, hoping to pass into enlightenment. I have taken the tests in strange places, in bar fights or the jungles of the Congo or in strange bedrooms. But I am, in all of these moments, waiting to see things, to see myself, in a new way. I want to learn geometry so that I will no longer be a slave to a world of random lines and angles. I want to know the area of my own life, how it is measured, even if the distance has at times been marked off in my own blood.

I snap awake. As if someone had lifted a curtain the world returns. *What the fuck was that*, I think. I will be happy, I decide, to finish my first competition awake.

. . .

I rise at five A.M. on a Tuesday in July. It is still dark outside in St. Augustine and the air smells like the rain that went through last night. I have a hot cup of mint tea with honey that congeals on the bottom of the mug like a candy. I pull a sweater over my T-shirt. It will be cold at altitude. I grab an apple. My gear is folded into a single bag that I lash to the front seat under the acro-belts. I crank hard on the ratchets, stuffing the bag down. The sun is up at six. I am gone at six-twenty. I am heading to my first competition and I expect the trip to take the better part of a day. The Extra has one large, forty-gallon fuel tank spread out inside the wings and a smaller one, for aerobatics, bolted near the engine. It holds just eight gallons and is designed to put fuel in the engine even when the plane is inverted or suffering high g-loads. For my cross-country flight I will fly only from the wing tanks if I can, putting in three-and-a-half-hour legs, saving the center as a reserve. Alan's final words to me. *You are as ready to go as fast as I've seen.* And: *Don't go on top. Don't fly above a cloud deck, even if the weather is clear there, even if the forecasters say it is a small deck.*

I have had nine days to master the plane, to grapple with the complexities of the competition sequence. I must be kidding myself. To compete now? I will be facing pilots with hundreds of hours, months of practice. Some of the figures I have flown five or six times. The easy ones. I've flown the entire sequence three times. And these were wobbly efforts, loaded with blemishes, such as weak, g-avoiding pulls through the bottoms of figures.

Getting to Oklahoma will be chore enough. The cross-country commutes in little aerobatic planes have driven more than a few pilots from the sport. Not the boredom—though that's bad enough, hour after hour of propeller noise in a cockpit built for seven-minute flights—but the possibility of disastrous surprises. The planes have no instruments for night flight or operations in bad weather, which makes slipping into a mistake very easy. You often are improvising from the moment of liftoff, climbing on top of cloud decks or racing below thunderheads. The sky holds limitless trouble. Say you elect to fly for a while "on top," climbing above a solid cloud layer to find clear skies. You have a theory you are testing, perhaps that the clouds will burn off as the day warms or that they will blow away well before you need to land. The gas needle slowly slips leftward, toward zero, while you test this theory. It is still lovely on top, above the clouds, but they are not breaking up. Maybe you turn around. The engine quits and suddenly you are left trying to decide if you should bail out or ride the plane blindly down toward the ground. Your life has become an opera.

The alternative isn't much better, *below* the clouds, scud-running. Dodging power lines and radio antennas at less than 1,000 feet. But you *must*. You fly along nervously squinting into the roan sky ahead, looking for the next bridge or high-tension line or building. Knowing all along that it is the bridge you don't see, the power line you can't make out, that has your name on it. "I once flew in a Pitts to a contest in Texas, flew all day, and I never got over 500 feet the whole time," guys like Clint McHenry, Loudenslager's friend and coach, will recall. It's a kind of macho game. *I once was down to twenty-five feet, surrounded by thunderstorms, out of gas.* Bullshit, you think. Then you see the leaves in their landing gear. "I'd find myself out over the woods somewhere and if my engine sputters I'm in the trees," said McHenry, bleeding common sense. "And I thought, you know you've been flying for all these thousands and thousands of hours. This is kind of stupid. But it is exciting."

Less exciting now that we have the satellites for navigation. But in the old days, with just a map! You really had to have an airport in your back pocket then. It was a kick. You don't get that from golf. But these crazy commutes, the suicide sprints between airports, were what pushed even a legend like Frank Price out of the game. They retired McHenry. You could be an aging champion like Joe Frasca, commuting back home from U.S. Nationals when your plane shreds up like lettuce in turbulence. You jump clear, reach gratefully for your chute, and pull. But you have undone the parachute's legstraps to get comfortable in the cockpit. The canopy slithers open above you, the jerk tears it off your back, and you watch it above like a kite as you plummet alone and cold into the ground. *Be scared to death of just getting there.* McHenry's survivor's words.

Almost immediately after I take off I am on top of a haze layer. The air is smooth here, clear. A wind pushes me from behind. I am at 8,500 feet, making time. *Don't fly on top.* I hear Alan. But I am not on top, I argue with myself. The clouds below are not clouds! From the side they may look like thick, ropy sheets of white foam, but when I look straight down they appear transparent, harmless. The sun is playing with me. It is low in the sky, striking the mist from the side, making it look rich as mortar. But I know it is meringue. I motor on. The fuel is burning away at ten gallons an hour. My engine exhaust temperature is 1,325 degrees. The propeller goes round 2,500 times a minute. Below me the old Indian towns of Florida stream past. I watch them on my map.

One hour. Two. There is a kind of peace to flying that is unknown in the back of a jetliner. You are just busy enough as a pilot to be living completely in the moment. Have you ever sat and watched a candle burn down to the bottom, seen the way time just decelerates? From time to time your mind will wander forward to the things that await you, but you are in no rush to get there. Below me the character of the cloud base is changing and I have all the time in the world to watch it. It is thicker than it was earlier, but also more broken up, like pieces of skin on milk. I roll the plane on a wing and look down, through the holes. If I need to land urgently, I can pick my way through to find an airport. I can see highways underneath, snaking through the hills of southern Georgia. There go the people to work. Do they look at the sky? Two-and-a-half hours pass. The broken deck has become solid. A quarter-tank left in the wings. A full tank in the center. An hour at least, an hour-and-a-half of gas. The weather ahead at Mobile reports clear, a bit of haze. It is an hour away. I'm making a gamble: The clouds have to loosen up. I can turn around if they don't.

The clouds thicken.

The wing tank needle hovers dangerously close to nothing now. I switch over to my center tank. The heavy white field continues below me. I can see nothing of the ground. In my mind an alarm sounds and I put the plane hard over on a wing and head back south. I return to the point where I had noticed the clouds dissolving a half-hour before and find that here, too, they have congealed into a soupy mess, victims of a cold north wind. There is no hole for me to pick through. I glance at my fuel. A half-hour left. Maybe three-quarters if I can count on the scraps left in the wing tanks. I do not feel like a virtuous man at the moment. I hit the radio. Calm.

"I need to find a clear field."

"Well, we just had a good departure out of Charlie-91," the voice says.

I fly with one hand, holding the stick between my knees as I page through my map until I find the field to the southeast, twenty miles away. Eight minutes. I punch the airport into the navigation computer and turn the plane toward it. It remains beautiful up where I am, above the clouds. The blue sky is untrammeled, the air like a lake at night.

The airport crawls toward me on the electronic map. I chop the power and begin a descent. I cannot see the field through the haze but it is at an altitude of 1,100 feet, the map says. I am descending from 6,500. I am not sure where the bases of the clouds are, but the tops appear to be at 3,000 or so. They are not breaking up and if they stay solid I will have to find a way through. I pass through 5,000 feet. 4,000. Below me the clouds at last begin tearing apart, like shredding wet paper. Green earth appears. Roads. Fields with farmers working. At three miles out, the airport is visible. I drop down to

1,000 feet. The fresh smell of growing wheat and cotton comes into the cockpit on the warm, wet air. I call in on the advisory frequency, bring the plane around for a landing, and settle gently onto the runway. With twenty minutes of fuel.

Oh, Charlie-91! One runway, tucked amid cornfields. An orange windsock, worn pink with age, hangs alongside the gas pumps. It moves as little as the land around me. The ten A.M. quiet. Alabama countryside is smeared with the immense eagerness of a summer morning. Everything is green. The flight office walls are papered with yellowed Learn to Fly posters. The linoleum floors are peeling. Old airplane magazines litter the desk. The cover of one says we are winning in Vietnam. I lie outside on my wing reading as the sky clears. It is almost as if this place were waiting for me to land. It springs to life to entertain me: the veteran rebuilding a biplane in a nearby hangar, the lineboy taking a break from his high school football two-a-day practices, the fried egg salad, the fresh peach tea with mint picked nearby. Who could have guessed there is so little space between right and wrong?

I am off again around noon and arrive safely over Weatherford, about sixty miles west of Oklahoma City along I-40, at around four, after a single fuel stop. You can feel the Oklahoma heat in the cockpit but you can also see it from the air, 103 degrees rippling over the ground like steam. Cops are out closing highways that are buckling in the inferno, totaling big rigs. My legs are cramping, the hamstring muscles pulling

insistently at my back. And I need a bathroom. The Weatherford airport has one runway, which runs north-south with the
prevailing wind. The trees in Oklahoma are bent north into
the wind from years of the southern blow. There is no control
tower. At five miles I call my turn inbound. "Welcome to
Weatherford," the radio says back. "One-seven is active and
the box is hot." The aerobatic box is filleted out of an old
field, jammed hard alongside the eastern border of the runway. I circle around to land, carefully flying my landing pattern over the western side of the field, away from the practice
area. To my right a Pitts Special is twisting in the sunlight,
working through a sequence. As I glance over, the pilot tucks
into a fast downward spin. On the ramp there are a dozen aerobatic planes: Pitts, Edges, Sukhois. Pilots stand around, half
undressed in clothes Nomexed against imagined future fires.
Someone is on the radio giving advice to the pilot in the box.
Faster. Tighter. Nice. The inevitable chorus. There is a pilot's
welcome, happy faces wandering over and offering help with
the plane.

I unstrap with one of those now unconscious rituals. I
undo my harness with my left hand, pull off the headset
quickly, and put my hand on the emergency canopy release.
Always the same sequence, because it is the one I will use if I
ever need to bail out in a hurry.

The Extra goes into the hangar shade. I fold my maps carefully, I lay my chute on the seat, and I wander down the ramp,
looking for a lift to the local motel. "Take one of the courtesy
cars," the airport manager says. Outside sits a 1977 Buick,
faded white, with the keys dangling in the ignition. Weather-

ford itself is little more than a truck stop, a three-block speed rush of concrete and Wal-Mart and gas stations. I grab a shower, some bad Mexican food, and a long night's sleep.

Competitions generally reach over Friday-Saturday-Sunday schedules, with Thursday reserved as a practice day. Sunday flying is curtailed to allow time to get home for Monday work. Thursday morning the airport is busier than when I left the night before. Thirty planes are spread out on the ramp. Pilots are casing their planes with tools, looking for problems. I push the Extra free from the group hangar and wipe down the wings with Lemon Pledge and an old rag. The leading edges of the wings are blackened with bugs picked up during my low approach into the airport. I work over the tail, cleaning traces of an oil leak.

A little after ten, as the day heats up, I take off and head out over the flat fields north of the airport to practice my known sequence. I make it halfway through before I have a problem with the split-S, a figure where I roll upside down and then pull through a seven-g half-loop, turning the plane around in the sky. I am using up too much altitude. On a sheet before the flight I have added up the altitude gain and loss on every figure, allocating just 800 feet for the split-S. It is easy to use more than that, the plane pointed earthward and picking up speed, and I am now using more than 1,000 feet. I kill the rest of my gas squeezing again and again through that one figure and the three-quarter loop that follows it, trying to get my net loss down to something manageable. If I drop more than 1,000 feet in the competition flight I will be too low to continue without a penalty. I bring it down to 700 feet lost; then 600. The cure is not surprising: a harder pull, more g's.

At eleven-forty, I have fifteen minutes to practice by myself in the aerobatic box. I take off and switch over to the competition frequency and call my arrival from the north. Another plane leaves to the south and turns hard for the field. I come in at 2,000 feet and am struck by how damn small the box looks. I pass through and come back around to start my sequence. I steal glances at the white corner markers on the ground. I am drifting east. I pull out of a spin in the middle of the box. I head straight up for the hammerhead, turn around, and come down 500 feet east of center. I finish the next figure out of the box altogether, pushed by a wind I hadn't expected. I try again from the start, hugging the west end of the box to compensate. Pull, push, spin, hammerhead, quarter-roll. I am out again. I try every correction I can think of, cheating the plane west with every pull, cutting my windward turns short to save space, furiously carving the wings into the wind the way you might knife-peel an orange. But I am still out. "A hell of a wind," says a German pilot who flies bush planes in Nigeria half the year. It wasn't just me.

But there are other worries. I am still plagued by grayed-out vision. To get onto a vertical line I have to pull up tight from horizontal flight, I have to make a corner in the sky. But the tight ascent is blinding me. As I pull into my hammerhead I can feel the blood pooling down to my ankles, slipping away from my brain and taking my awareness along for the ride. So

I set my upline blindly, on the verge of blackout, flying by instinct. I cannot make out anything at all. I swivel my head to the left as if I were going to look out over the wing, but of course, I can't see a thing. It is like phantom limb syndrome. My sight is gone, but I keep moving my head around as if everything were clear, as if I saw sky instead of a little gray tube. After a few seconds on my back in the sky, the g-loads lighten and my vision returns. I can finally check my alignment. But I am never lined up right, the way I would be if I could watch the whole affair unfolding. So I make small corrections, pushing the nose into place. It's distracting. The kind of thing judges will mark down. I am desperate to keep my blood pressure up, to help my heart. I find a taco stand in town and sit down for two hours of Gatorade and guacamole and chicken tacos. I buy some salt pills at the local drugstore and swallow eight before bed.

Friday morning is cloudy, the first overcast day in a week or more. Overhead the sky mottles and then clears. Someone posts the flight order. I am third. It is not the worst position—first—but it is not far enough down the list to provide any education. The pilots behind me will use my flight to judge their wind correction ideas. I will have to figure out my own. The planes are rolled onto the ramp in flight order, tucked into one another like pieces of a puzzle. The line is a football field long, fifteen-plus planes. The judges are shuttled to stands on one end of the box. The starter comes to the first pilot and gives a thumbs-up. I am standing on the ramp with the man who is flying just ahead of me, a flight school owner from Colorado. He seems unbeatable: a fancier plane than mine, more experience. I will beat him, I insist to myself. In fact, he zeros his flight with an error and I will beat him. He passes me a breath mint. "Something for your dry mouth." I take it, smiling. "Don't worry," says David Martin, the Texas-based Unlimited pilot, who has wandered by to give me moral support, "it will get drier." *Don't finish last*, I say to myself.

The first plane coughs awake, kicking dirt over the tarmac and into the crowd of pilots. The starter wanders by my plane. Cliff. It is my turn. "Okay," Cliff says, "get saddled." I climb in and he does his standard prestart check, running his practiced eyes over my plane and me. He can ground me with one word. Starters have been known to ground pilots who appear too nervous, who make silly mistakes in preflight. They are the last line of safety and approach their jobs with the seriousness of cops. My belts are secure. I flip the master power switch to check the gas. There is enough for twenty minutes of flight. "Fire up," Cliff says, making a mark on his clipboard. I lock the canopy, prime the engine, hit the ignition. The engine turns over a few times and then dies. I work the checklist again: mixture, throttle, fuel pump, magnetos. A limp cranking noise. The engine won't catch. I am wet with sweat in the hot cockpit. A dozen planes wait behind me. I try again. Nothing. The battery.

It is possible to start an airplane without a battery by spinning the prop through by hand until the engine catches. Extras are notoriously difficult to hand-prop. David Martin, who has more time in Extras than I have total time, jogs back over and a fast talks me through the details, yelling them through my tiny cockpit window. As I hold the magnetos open, he runs in front of my plane and begins pulling the prop around. "Contact," he says. "Contact," I shout back as I engage the magnetos. Paul Donner, another experienced pilot, runs over to help as well. "Contact," David says. I turn the key. Nothing. Paul begins spinning the prop backward to clear the cylinders, then forward again. He moves gingerly. This is a fast way to lose a hand if the engine grabs suddenly. "Contact," he says. As he spins again, the engine catches. I slam the gas in and put the fuel boost on. One cylinder at a time the engine wakes up. Cooler air streams back into the cockpit and my heart slows a bit.

I retighten my belts and taxi forward for a test runup on the engine. I pass though a quick electrical system check. No bounce on the electrical meter from anything. The symptoms of a dead alternator, and an explanation for my battery problem. I will fly anyway. I take the active runway, hit the throttle, and am quickly airborne. I pull up and around to the northwest, into a small holding area over a golf course where I wait to be cleared into the box. No warm-up maneuvers are permitted. I use the hold time to fly a few straight lines over roads, watching which way the wind pushes me and how fast. The slight breeze from the south is fine improvement over yesterday's easterly tornado. After five minutes I am cleared into the box.

I leave the holding area and fly south to make a broad left turn. I roll inverted to test my belts. Plonk! My fuel strainer, a five-inch-long plastic tube that I use to check for water in the gas before each flight, rattles out of its container and onto the canopy above my head. I make a weak left-handed stab for it as I roll back upright, but it grazes my fingers and disappears under my seat. I feel around furiously, dropping the nose of the plane as I fumble, but my seat straps are holding me so tightly I cannot bend fully over to grope. If the fuel strainer isn't under my seat it has likely rolled back through the tail section. It may well be jammed up against the rod that controls the rudder and elevator. Pilots have been killed or have had to bail out after small objects floated loose and fixed into an evil place in their controls. Screwdrivers, bolts, pens. If it is not in the tail section, it could be somewhere else, waiting to pop loose. The smart thing to do is land, get out, and make sure the damn thing isn't in my tail.

I enter the box for my sequence and begin to fly. I am not sure why. Perhaps after the hung start the last thing I want to do is land and confess that now my fuel strainer is loose. It would be a zero for the flight, an even sharper blow to my machismo. I don't think the decision through. As I flip into a spin, nothing out of the ordinary happens. The plane feels fine. The stick is firm in my hand. The plane responds to every command. Wherever the strainer is, the devil's work is still beyond it. There are another ten figures ahead. I recover from the spin with a hard pull. The stick hiccups a little as I pull back. Is something caught? I press over into my next figure with inelegant paranoia. The rest of the sequence unfolds like a one-legged waltz, my uncertainty visible in every figure. The plane responds to my every thought, even fear.

I circle and land. I taxi back to the ramp, hop out, and when no one is looking walk back to the tail of the plane. Under the tail is a clear Lucite panel installed so that I can peek inside the plane to check for obstructions before each flight. As I crouch down and look through the tiny window, I see the fuel strainer propped between two pieces of metal, two inches from disaster. I unscrew the panel and pluck the strainer out with my fingers. I close my eyes for a second.

What got him? "Loose fuel strainer in the cockpit."

The day erodes. I am out on the judges line after my flight, helping to judge another group of pilots. "You know, he really reminds me of John Nagy," my judging partner says apropos of another pilot. The sky is quiet between flights and I have been sitting, idly fingering my fuel strainer. "Know Nagy?" he continues. "Big, bearish guy. Terrific pilot. I'll miss him at Nationals." I know John. I almost bought his plane a few years ago, a 1970s-era Czech Zlin, checkerboarded red and white on the nose. We flew together one spring Sunday in Pennsylvania. Nagy was in his mid-fifties and had restored the plane himself. He said he wanted to buy a boat. But you could see his heart wasn't in it.

"Why won't he be at Nationals?" I ask.

"He was killed last week."

I look at him. He is a kid. Maybe twenty. No lines on his face. Eyes clear as the sky. "They don't know what happened. His passenger managed to bail out, but John was killed in the crash. You know, it's been a rough year for them. His wife was almost killed dead-sticking a Pitts in. He was a great guy, though."

I sat there on the flight line, then returned to my hotel room after sunset. Very quiet. I was haunted. The hung start. The fuel strainer. Nagy dead in a plane I had almost bought. The whole point of this was to be transported closer to the truth, right? To virtue? A dialogue with myself. Well, here it was. Who said it would always be easy or pleasant? The joyful pure light of flight itself was hard to make out now. It could barely cut the dimness of my fears. The place I was intent on visiting was the frontier of my own mind. I *had* found new places there. They were ugly.

It was strange after the weeks of baking heat in Oklahoma to have two cool, dark mornings backed onto each other. But the next day, more clouds. We arrived for a seven A.M. briefing already impatient. Some local Jaycees gamely forked out hot pancakes in the cool air. The news was simple: we would wait for the clouds to clear. Pilots wandered off to the airport's ratty lounge and collapsed around a TV showing a silenced weather channel. The commentary was irrelevant. A large cell of thunderstorms was scooting ominously toward us from the west. The station kept replaying it, like a fumble at a football game or a home run.

The night had cleared my demons, as it often does, and I was eager to fly again. After my first flight I was in next-to-last place and angry. I was not out by much, just a handful of points from the pilots ahead of me. I had zeroed one maneuver. I suspected that I had failed to hold the "point" of a two-point roll long enough, making it look like a continuous roll—enough to get no score for the figure. A "zero." A rookie error. I had no "outs," though. The whole sequence had been tight inside the box.

Maybe there was a part of me that didn't want to fly. The part noodling John Nagy's death, remembering the fuel strainer bouncing away into my tail. *You will almost kill yourself once every hundred hours of flying*, goes one saw. I had had mine. A three-dollar piece of plastic. A lot of mistakes you make once. Sometimes you only live to make them once. But most of the time you can scoot away to fly another day, a day when you go to Wal-Mart and buy some velcro to keep the fuel strainer in place.

One older American aerobatic pilot likes to tell the story of the day he mustered for his WWII Air Corps training. "On the same day you were recruited to be pilots," the commanding officer explained to the assembled men at their very first briefing, "the Army also recruited another man. His job is to kill you and make it look like an accident." My first flight instructor tried to drive this home by screwing something loose on our plane before occasional flights without warning me. I had to pick up the danger during my preflight checks. The missing alternator belt, say, or some water in a gas tank. I approached the plane looking for sabotage, as if I were flying from occupied lands. Had that fuel strainer downed me, it would have been a victory for the guy trying to make it look like an accident.

The Nagy thing bothered me more. The vivid image of the man, in that jewelbox airplane, smashing into the ground as his passenger bailed out to safety was perplexing and upsetting. But this is the mix that characterizes most aviation accidents. Very few arrive without the perplexity, with a clear sense of "Okay, that was really stupid." There are some: the non-instrument-rated pilot who loads his family into a poorly maintained plane and heads into an ice storm. But most of the crashes, particularly the ones that kill your friends, rankle a bit in their inscrutability. They seem almost deliberately opaque, darkened by fate so that we cannot completely understand them. They are lessons to us, of course. But not the Socratic kind, not the kind that leave behind a clear moral or a repeatable piece of wisdom. These lessons simply haunt.

By two-thirty, small blue patches appear in the gray sheet above us. The thunder cell turns south. In the random draw, I pulled the very last slot. With the late start, I will likely start my sequence right at dusk, which means I'll need to stay a little lower than usual to make sure I can be seen. I also discover, in looking over the starting sheet, that I will be flying after an airshow pilot who is in competition for just about the first time since he slammed his plane into the ground at about 250 miles an hour in front of a crowd. "I'm just trying to see how my back will hold up against the g's," he says as we wait to start.

I am cleared to roll at about seven-thirty, as the sky bleeds into the orange and purple streaks of a midwestern twilight. It is a lovely, smooth night and as I pull free of the runway, the airplane feels lively and fresh in my hands. At 3,000 feet I orbit quietly in a holding area. There is almost no noise on the box frequency now, just the occasional comment that a pilot is in or has just left the box. The airplane is running well and the air is so cool that there are no bumps. The fading sun catches at a few high clouds, flash-painting them pink for an instant. The radio crackles for me.

I roll the plane smoothly over in a tight turn and establish myself on a line parallel to the box. I'll fly this out a half mile south and then turn in as fast as I can to start my sequence. I roll inverted to check my belts. All firm. Nothing loose in the cockpit. I snap upright again and turn inbound. I settle onto a straight line in and push the nose over to pick up speed. I can see a strong wind vibrating the trees east of the field. I put the plane over to that side of the box as a compensation. The nose goes down sharply and fast as I push forward. The airspeed builds and as the flow over the wings accelerates I can feel the controls stiffen, a sign the plane is ready for aerobatic flight. In my peripheral vision, I try to catch the ground mark that shows the edge of the box. It glows white in the twilight. I am abeam. I rock my wings to signal the sequence start and pull five g's to level at 2,000 feet. I pull hard to vertical. My head is lively with joy.

The flight is over quickly, like shooting through a tunnel in a train. The figures flow out of my stick one after another. There is no thinking about form or shape or timing, just the mechanics of flying and a tickling sensation of lightness. I make a few ostentatious points for the judges, jamming on my rudder during the half-Cuban I had zeroed, marking each point of the roll. And I hold my vertical downlines a bit longer, patiently watching the earth come up, squaring the shape of the figures. There is a lingering quality to the flight even in its most violent moments. I pull out of my last roll screaming, my heart open with joy. I hear my happiness flood out over the sound of the engine. "Whoooooopeee." I am unbound.

I land and taxi in. The kindergarten-aged daughter of the airport manager wanders up with a frozen Dr. Pepper for me. *Was Dr. Pepper on every menu in Oklahoma?* I had joked with her dad earlier in the day, so he has arranged this post-flight reward. I pull off my parachute. I sit down beside my plane on the sun-warmed asphalt and sip at the icy soda. In three days I have learned so much. I have started to see the corners of my own virtues. It is not unlike the moment in the Meno when Socrates reflects on his own life. "One thing I would fight for to the end," he says solemnly, "both in word and deed if I were able—that if we believed that we must try to find out what is not known, we should be better and braver."

I have finished in tenth place for the flight, eleventh overall, and I collect the trophy for Best First-Time Competitor. Lower than I would like, but that first flight was unrecoverable. My box position in the high winds, a couple of the judges tell me, was an impressive thing. I flew the final known with no zeros. No polish, either, pinching the tops of loops and dishing sideways slightly on rolls. But I am a braver and less idle man for the effort.

The summer of '77 was a
kind of Paleolithic era
for extreme sports.

The summer of '77 was a kind of Paleolithic era for extreme sports. A crucial evolutionary jump hovered ahead, just visible. Extreme sports were about to begin to learn to walk on two legs, they were going to start along that road from cult to main street. A young University of North Carolina graduate student named Janice Proger spent the best part of that summer moving through the migrant camps of rafters, parachutists, rock climbers, and hang-gliders who—liberally aided by marijuana—were making this revolution in sports. She was beginning her field research for her doctoral dissertation: "A Description of Stimulus-Seeking in Sport According to Flow Theory." Proger carried with her a stack of mimeographed sheets on each of which was typed a list of sixty statements. Statement 1 was: "I sometimes worry about my abilities to meet the challenges of a situation prior to an event, but that disappears once I get into the activity." Number 60 was: "I never feel self-conscious when I am doing my thing in sport. I just float along and have fun." The sixty statements were the heart of her Ph.D. project. They were going to provide a road map into the brains of extreme athletes. They would explain, she hoped, why we take risks.

Every time Proger found a willing subject, she handed them the sixty statements and an index card on which they could rate the statements on a scale of one to seven, from MOST LIKE ME to LEAST LIKE ME. She found no shortage of takers. On cloudy days, parachutists happily stopped to indicate if they would "rather forgo an event than suffer the anxiety that results from conditions far below my experience." (No chance.) Kayakers told her if they felt that "my sport needs no other justification than itself." (Yes.) Seventy-seven men and women, aged eighteen to seventy-seven, rated themselves. One kayaking club manager wrote Proger that his members would have jumped to be included in a study of high-risk sports, but lamented that they were just at the moment "too busy out 'high-risking' themselves."

Proger was exploring a subject that had long troubled psychologists: Why do people get so excited about risks that generate no reward? Why do we take them in the first place? We ride cars and motorcycles and horses faster than we need. We drink too much. We have more sex than evolution demands, sometimes in ways that wreck our lives. And some of us ride, drink, and fuck far, far more than we need. Was this some flaw in our operating system? Could it be debugged? Psychology was supposed to be constrained at least a little by Darwin's evolutionary laws, by the premise that really absurdly stupid behavior should have been weeded out of the gene pool millennia ago. That scientific notion had a damn hard time explaining parachute jumping.

But then you looked at history and, hell, the course of human events, that magnificent thing we studied as kids, was just plastered with this kind of mortal idiocy. Achilles sprinting around a Trojan beach after Patroklos' death, looking for redemption on the tip of someone else's sword. Or Socrates reaching out for that bowl, pressing himself toward eternity. The Greeks called all of this *akrasia*, a sickness, an unstoppable impulse toward self-destruction. That it afflicted some of the people we most admired just made it a more fascinating problem.

Of course Freud couldn't resist it. He struggled with the problem, writing around it again and again before finally concluding with this Theory of All Risk: We are all neurotics. Some of us are just more neurotic than others. Humans have such a keen sense of mortality, he explained, that we sometimes want to seek it out early. We hear our heart beat. We cannot help but wonder what it will be like when the sound stops. So, at times, we do things that let us at least feel death's curves, things that make our hearts skip a beat. For some people, he explained, there was something to enjoy in anticipating death. To the Freudian mind, a dangerous wind in our hair makes us feel alive because it reminds us that we will not always be so. Most of us, he said, can control our taste for this mortal preview, but for a few of our brothers and sisters, cursed by neuroses, it becomes irresistible. Death-love, he called it. These folks, if we wanted to graft on the modern lingo, are obsessive-compulsives, he suggests, but instead of touching the stove to see if it is hot, instead of checking and rechecking the door to see if it is locked, they insist on seeing how close they can get to death without dying. Often they lose the bet. They are cleaned off motorcycles rounding corners. They push one too many needles in their arms.

You might imagine a kind of hierarchy of early deaths. At

the top of this ranking there are glorious deaths. Or deaths that at least seem glorious, for causes bigger than our own satisfaction. In battle, for instance, or defending your family and your honor. These are cases where our idealism overwhelms our sense of self. Saint Exupéry, the great French pilot and writer, after a lifetime of narrowly missing death-by-plane-accident went to the Spanish civil war in the early 1930s to watch people who sought death avidly, with patriotism in their eyes. "How does it happen that men are sometimes willing to die?" he wondered in his journal of that trip. But death by needless risk? These acts are pretty low on the hierarchy of self-death. Here the logic of human survival starts to break. Where was the nobility? Why on earth would anyone strap themselves into a plane and heave it around a few hundred feet off the ground? All of psychological history argued against this kind of behavior.

Men and women are supposed to be programmed to reduce stress. How else to explain the passion for civilization and its luxuries? For warmth and love? For stability? For nearly a century, the psychological world puffingly concluded that Freud was right: people who sniffed too long at dangerous risks must be damaged, they must have lost that crucial ability to observe death without embracing it. We were all dying from the moment we were born, of course, but some of us are doing it faster than others. Some of us are walking suicides.

"'Emotionally healthy' individuals prefer security and safety," one shrink, B. C. Ogilvie, wrote in a 1974 summary of conventional wisdom about this stew of risk, life, and mind. He summarized the neuralgia of risk-takers with painful specificity. They must, he said, "suffer from one or more of the following mental pathologies: counter-phobic reactions, fear displacement, super masculinity or an unconscious death wish." Those happy-looking hang-glider pilots? Super-masculine. (Don't ask about the women pilots, please.) The kayaker? A counter-phobic reaction to a deep fear of water, probably induced in the neighborhood pool at age six. Any species that naturally embraced risk was doomed. Perhaps among our ancestors there was a tribe that liked hand-feeding dinosaurs. They didn't survive to tell anyone about it. The few risk-takers who swam out of the evolutionary soup were, in this view, anomalous psychological gaffes, rounding errors on the evolutionary scale. And as messed up as a finger painting. "Risk-taking behavior often occurs when individuals attempt to prove their courage, audacity, or capacity to achieve results in the face of dangerous elements," wrote one Freudian. "Basic to this mechanism is a need to improve self-esteem and/or self-confidence by accepting risk. Individuals may engage in a certain amount of impulsive and risk-taking behavior because they wish to destroy or injure themselves."

Is it any surprise then that the best research on risk-taking is filed in most libraries next to the larger, more colorful literature on suicide? "Self-destruction occurs in many ways," Norman Faberow writes ominously in the introduction to *The Many Faces of Suicide*. "Some obvious, some disguised, but always hastening, in one way or another, one's own death." And occasionally, he may as well have added, involving airplanes, parachutes, kayaks, or rock-climbing gear.

. . .

And then came the space men. The NASA researchers started breaking the risk china, the carefully preserved Freudian heritage, with study after study. The worry, they said, was that any cowboy crazy enough to shoot into space would be too damn nuts to do any good once he was up there. In 1968 they slotted race car drivers against bowlers and studied the hell out of them. Did the race car drivers have bigger hearts, more testosterone in their systems, did they peg the wrong end of the scale on the head tests? No. There was almost no perceptible difference. From a mental-health perspective, your average bowler and your average race car driver looked pretty much the same. And at the same time these studies were coming out, the once canonical idea that humans act only in order to purge their lives of unpleasantness (building a house, making money) or to satisfy our biological needs (fill in your own blank) was being eroded by volumes of research. Hell, it was being eroded by common sense. Once people satisfied their basic needs, they sought out all kinds of stimulation for no apparent instrumental purpose. Where did skiing get anyone other than down a hill? Art? You could, the researchers began to suggest, think of these choices as an extra need beyond basic survival, as a need for stimulation. Everyone's optimal level of stimulation was different, the research discovered, but the desire for it was as universal, and maybe as necessary, as the desire to eat.

Research into "sensation-seeking" began in a surprising place: sensory-deprivation chambers, dark rooms where sensations of all kinds were discouraged if not prohibited. In the early 1950s, researchers at the University of California were trying to study what happened to people when you blocked out all the sensory evidence that they were alive: sound, sight, taste, even touch. The idea was to remove influence from the human brain and then stir it back in, one ingredient at a time, to see how the mind reacted. But while those experiments were under way, the researchers spotted a problematic quirk among their research subjects. "We noticed," one scientist wrote, "that the people volunteering for these studies, as well as those volunteering for a hypnosis experiment, did not look or act like the typical college student volunteer of that time." The crew-cut kids strolling around the Eisenhower-era campus happily chatting about football and cheerleaders weren't the ones signing up for the deprivation chambers. Who was? Ads that promised some sort of novel or unusual experiences such as hallucination in sensory-deprivation chambers drew high-sensation seekers out of the student population like a magnet. They drew nonconformists. And when finally bolted into their isolation chambers, these volunteers didn't have much tolerance for any experiment that involved low or no sensation. They couldn't keep still. They were restless. *Hey, I signed up to hallucinate!* They had more random movements than normal kids. They ignored requests to stop moving. "Please stop touching yourself," the scientists would intone over a speaker as their overamped frat-boy subject patted his stomach or clacked his tongue with boredom. As sensory-deprivation subjects, these kids were the worst imaginable sample. Inadvertently, the scientists had found a way to self-select one of the most perplexing groups in the psychological landscape. But as a chance to begin exploring why some people seek more stimulus than others, they were a Rosetta stone.

The human brain covets challenges, even needs them in order to stay limber. The world changes, and a mind that can't adjust is doomed. This is, in a way, the attraction of crossword puzzles or mazes or mystery novels. They are little challenges that we use to keep our neural pathways well lubricated. The brain rewards us for these exercises with a burst of serotonin, the chemical that enhances mood. But in early studies of high-sensation seekers, something strange emerged from these innocent mental exercises. Take the maze puzzle. Imagine a maze designed with several possible routes in and out. If you give the multiple-route maze problem repeatedly to the same 1,000 people, most of them will pick one path and trace it again and again. It's like driving the same route home every day. But a minority—the high-sensation seekers—will instinctively change their route almost every time they get the puzzle. They change at a far greater rate than their "normal" peers. "Some of them," wrote a researcher who tried this experiment, echoing his frustrated colleagues with the sensory-deprivation tanks, "will draw a route that goes outside the maze, despite instructions to stay within it!"

What was driving these outside-the-line subjects? There were some biological clues. For instance, it was possible to sort people into categories by their tolerance for stimulation.

Using a series of tests that rated people's reaction to loud noises, bright colors, or big surprises, German researchers were able to divide a test group into people with "strong" and "weak" nervous systems. Once they'd done this, they started comparing how each group reacted to the same set of stimuli. People with "strong" nervous systems tended to absorb less from their environments than those with "weak" nerves, who tended to amplify every hiccup into a major event.

It was as if people had a preset dial rigged to each of their senses. The spicy bratwurst that nauseated one group tasted a little bland to the other. Loud Wagner arias gave one group headaches while hardly disturbing the sleep of the other. Strong-nervous-system "reducers" rounded sensation down. As a result, the scientists postulated, that group sought stimulation in increasingly complex, interesting, and intense encounters with their environment. These "reducers," one researcher found, reported that they "expose themselves quite frequently to intense, complex situations in their ongoing social activities and avoid dull stimulus activities." The addiction to action spread across a subject's entire life, a nice even coat of adrenaline on their twitchy muscles. "I have concluded," wrote one pioneer in risk theory, "that sensation seeking is a general trait that is not restricted to any one sensory modality. The high-sensation seekers are likely to have not just one but any number of adventurous tastes from an eagerness to try risky activities such as sky-diving to a desire for a variety of sexual partners." The folks with weak nerves, "augmenters," found solace instead in simple, dull, and quiet situations.

The researchers also noticed something else: high-sensation seekers tended to appraise risks differently. In fact, they tended dramatically to underestimate risk. And even when groups of high- and low-sensation seekers appraised a situation in generally the same way—*Yes, jumping from that three-story building into the pool is risky*—the high-sensation seekers contemplated the activity with actual pleasure. The low-sensation seekers felt nothing but anxiety.

This went a long way to explaining what the Freudians had labeled neuroses. It wasn't that there was something wrong with risk-takers, rather that they experienced the world differently. This was especially true when you studied them over long periods of time. Among sensation seekers, the most intense joy came from taking risks again and again— preferably risks that were bigger each time. Once sensation-seeking subjects had mastered skiing, they wanted to start jumping. Once they had mastered jumping, they wanted to do tricks in midair. Then they wanted to do them on steeper slopes. They wanted to ski faster. To continue to achieve "optimal" levels of stimulation they needed to make their activities harder. Studies of parachutists in the 1960s found that as they gained experience they were able to replace fear with pleasure. But fear had to be present to begin with. It was the displacement that made the joy possible. The catch was that some of the most experienced jumpers, the ones with hundreds of jumps, found themselves chasing that high by pulling their rip cords lower and lower in the sky, waiting longer with every jump. Waiting, inevitably, *too* long sometimes.

This was the trait, this deadly ratcheting of danger, that made risk-taking so compulsive and ugly. "A finding relevant in self-destructive behavior from the parachuting research," one scientist wrote, "is that some highly experienced sport parachutists appear to have become addicted to jumping." Then, launching a rear-guard for the Freudians, he concluded that the finding "suggests that certain destructive lifestyles may be difficult to change because they reduce anxiety stemming from unrecognized or otherwise intractable sources." Bad day at the office? Jump out of a plane. To researchers on drug and gambling and alcohol addiction this all sounded familiar. The difference between a kayak and a crack pipe was, for them, hard to see.

The first credible answer to this worldview came in 1974 from Mihaly Csikszentmihalyi, a Czech-born researcher at the University of Chicago. Csikszentmihalyi (his friends called him Mike C. to maintain their linguistic sanity) developed a theoretical model that explained human choices not in terms of mental mechanistics—"my father was an asshole, therefore I'm a fighter pilot"—but in the language of play.

Csikszentmihalyi asked his subjects to wear pagers and would buzz them in the middle of the day, randomly. *Sit down and rate how happy you are right now*, they were told. *Now describe what you are doing.* He found an exact correlation between happiness and what he called *flow*, a state of complete absorption. Some factory workers, toiling at mind-numbing jobs, managed flow for themselves by setting little games in their heads. "How many bolts can I turn this hour?" Workers who just looked at themselves as human screwdrivers were unhappy. Those who set—and met—challenges were as happy as the brain surgeons he studied.

His essential idea was that people derived joy from how they related to the environment around them, not from some preestablished set of mental constraints. Our happiness, he said, is determined mostly by the relationship between our skills and our world. To be happy, the skills we have and challenges we face should synchronize so that we face challenges that are just a little too hard for us, tough enough to keep us engaged but not so hard that we are constantly failing. Moving together, Csikszentmihalyi argued, this balance of challenge and skill provides leverage for joyful life. We are in the flow when they match up. When they don't, trouble ensues. Confronted with challenges too great or too simple, we slide into anxiety or boredom. A speech before five people we don't know can terrify us. Sitting alone can bore us stiff. The ideal state is somewhere in between, a Goldilocks place where we have in the same moment just enough skills and challenge.

But while one person might find enough challenge by working on the *New York Times* Sunday crossword, another needed mouth-parching risk. Physical danger provided a kind of centering of attention. The more some people were required to concentrate to stay alive, the happier they were. But in that flow state, there was heaven. No sense of self. A loss of any perception of time. Total freedom from worry and complete immersion in the moment. "All the hang-ups I have are momentarily obliterated," one rock climber told researchers. What risk was too much for that result?

For Csikszentmihalyi and a generation of researchers like Proger, flow was an improvement on Freud's nasty collision of pleasure and pain. It made it okay to take risks. It made it healthy, even. At least one tribe of neo-Freudian psychologists did rebel, arguing that Csikszentmihalyi had simply identified a new class of neuroses, a special sickness endemic among risk-takers. This flowlike passion to live in the moment, to transcend worry, was really just another route toward suicide, they said, every bit as neurotic as manic-depression, though admittedly more fun. Ascensionism, the disease was called, or more cleverly "The Icarus Complex": a desire to move above the earth, a flawed sense of superiority often, one researcher snidely noted, correlated with bed-wetting. Csikszentmihalyi fought back. "Like all explanations that try to reduce enjoyment to a defensive ploy against anxieties, this one misses the point. It is more worthwhile to consider acts that bring enjoyment as signs of health not disease."

This was what seduced Janice Proger's Ph.D. subjects and sent her out into that hot summer to talk to risk-takers. Sports seemed a natural place to test flow theory. "Almost all channels for the expression of eudaimonism—war, village donnybrooks, the struggle against nature—are now blocked," one psychologist had observed in 1968. "Those that remain [are] risky sports."

What those summer-of-'77 kids were looking for wasn't death, but a sense of pleasure. They were after the high that came from mastery and drawn to the total immersion their sports offered. Proger found her athletes weren't taking risks in exchange for financial reward or fame or even, since most of the sports didn't have any formal win-lose competitions, for victory. There were no lucrative endorsement contracts, no television-sized personalities. They were doing it for the sheer joy of managing something hard, for the pleasure that came with absorption.

And none of Proger's subjects described what they were doing as dangerous. They even quibbled with the language of her questionnaire. "I do not believe I participate in a high-risk sport," one hang glider scribbled into the margins of the card he handed back in. "I must dispel your characterization of soaring as being a 'high-risk' sport," a glider pilot complained. "In fact it has one of the best safety records in aviation." Then, in an aside, "We are frequently mistaken [for] hang gliding, which is *a whole other ballgame.*" Proger's high-riskers saw themselves as doing everything they could to minimize risk. "In all activities, equipment was ritually checked," she wrote. "Proper instruction was emphasized. When weather conditions were questionable and the environmental factors could not be controlled by the sportsperson's skills, lift planes remained idle while parachutists waited for enough ceiling to jump."

Flow helped explain the individual choice of risk, but the job of making an evolutionary case for risk-taking would have to wait nearly twenty years after Proger's study, until scientists began understanding the chemistry of the brain. Still, there were hints of some chemical link even in 1977. An early 1970s study examined karate champions and mountain climbers and found few of the chemical traces of pain in their blood, even after they'd been subjected to things that would floor most people. Inside the brain itself, it seemed, highly individualized chemical reactions governed how and when we took risks and how we reacted to them.

The idea was synthesized in the early 1990s, when Frank Farley, a researcher at the University of Wisconsin, began grouping extreme athletes into what he called "Type-T" personalities." The T stood for thrills. Farley believed that the propensity for risk was biological. It should be, he reasoned, as detectable as dyslexia. Farley divided the world into two categories: "big T" thrill-seekers and "little T" thrill-avoiders. Big Ts prefer uncertainty, novelty, high risk, ambiguity, and low structure. Small Ts prefer the couch.

Farley found both a good and bad side to Big T personalities. The good news was that these thrill-seekers tended to be more creative, they wanted to see the world differently and pushed hard to change their environment, often for the better. Creativity, Farley argued, takes place on the very edge of uncertainty. From an evolutionary standpoint, this link was important because it explained why Big Ts lingered in our gene pool. Instead of being weeded out by their stupid, risky behavior, Big Ts very often found smarter ways to do things. The risks they took only sometimes manifested themselves as bungee jumping. Other times Big Ts postulated that the earth was round, that light speed was relative, that music need not be based on a twelve-tone scale. Big Ts invented cars and medicines, revolutionized farming and economics. They had a genius for seeing the world fresh.

But the same genes that produced a desire to innovate could also create an urge to immolate. "Risk-taking behavior," one colleague of Farley's argued, "is a major public health problem in our country. It includes gambling, accident-prone behavior, suicidal behavior, and disease-promoting activities. The costs in terms of human life, suffering, financial burden and lost work hours are enormous." Farley called these destructive twitches a result of Type-T negative behavior. In one experiment, he and his colleagues pretested young boys going into a mental institution to see if they could predict who was more likely to try to escape. Type-Ts, the kids who sought thrills, made seven times more escape attempts. Drug taking and sexual activity also correlated with the thrill-seeking personality. Researching lost virginity—"First Encounters of the Close Kind," Farley labeled the study—he found that Type-Ts had sex a year earlier than their peers. And once started, they kept going, racking up more sexual partners and more experiences-per-partner. Ts, Farley found, tended to be attracted to each other. Breeding, presumably, another generation of promiscuous, drug-addled parachutists before moving on to a new partner.

Farley's research made big waves in public health. It suggested, for instance, that appealing to Type-Ts to stop their behavior because it was risky was like trying to convince people with eating disorders to quit eating because food tasted good. With Ts, saying something was risky was an inducement, not a warning. Big Ts were hungry for risk. In some cases, Farley found, danger-based anti-AIDS campaigns had the reverse of the intended effect, encouraging dangerous sex instead of stopping it. The chance of acquiring the disease through sex was part of the thrill for some of his subjects. Fortunately, the number of such respondents was very low—about 10 percent—but it captured a larger problem. Type-Ts move to the rhythm of a very personal thrill meter. Pleasure and risk are often one and the same. When Farley correlated thrill-seeking with crimes, he found that more adventurous crimes like robbery and rape attracted bigger thrill-seekers. The desire for risk and sensation was so pervasive in some people that it made even punishment problematic. Jailing a risk-loving teenager for two months for drunk driving was sometimes counterproductive. For the wrong kind of teen, two months in jail was a blast.

He also argued that jail might not be a good solution anyhow. The key was to find ways to replace negative thrill-seeking with positive thrill-seeking. Why punish an impulse that couldn't be curbed any more than hunger could be? Taking troubled adolescents on Outward Bound–style programs was better than punishing them. It filled their taste for risk in a healthy way, like swapping Big Macs for stir-fry. You can't change Type-Ts. The chemical impulse for risk may fade as we age, but it will always be there. Therapy, punishment, all of the traditional stuff just didn't work, Farley argued. It might be possible to medicate the taste for risk. And that might be desirable in some cases. But if Csikszentmihalyi was right, trying to get rid of it altogether was also a mistake. There is nothing wrong or sick about taking risks. The problem is that for some of us, risk can kill.

. . .

In 1974, in one of the very first studies of risk and mind, B. C. Ogilvie and C. C. Pool interviewed a handful of aerobatic pilots and developed a profile of the best competition pilots, and separated the winners from losers. Their conclusions about the winners were summarized by pilot and Ph.D. Fred Delacerda:

> The results revealed that this particular group of aerobatic pilots were extreme introverts, yet they viewed social status as being important; however, they derived satisfaction from personal achievement rather [than] social approval. They enjoyed the spotlight, but in a quiet manner, with inner reaction rather than outward exuberance. Hence they tended to seek activities that reinforced status and, despite being part of a group, tended to be self-sufficient.
>
> The test data revealed these aerobatic pilots to be ambitious, organized and tenacious. While they showed concern with detail and planning ahead, they also demonstrated a definite trend towards exhibitionism, often doing the unconventional, particularly if it meant being noticed by others.
>
> These pilots ranked independence as a strong need and were not especially interested in others. This strong sense of independence allowed them to criticize those in authority. They were highly opinionated, not timid about expressing their opinion, and did not readily accept challenges to their opinions.

[They] were cool, reserved, facing reality in a calm and deliberate manner. As self-reliant, no-nonsense individuals they were enterprising, decisive and imperturbable. There was overwhelming evidence of perfectionism, with a need to live by a system. There was a drive to be successful, to accomplish something of significance. In essence, these pilots were extremely driven individuals.

The highest-ranked
American aerobatic pilot
in the world is unemployed.

The highest-ranked American aerobatic pilot in the world is unemployed. For the better part of the last twenty years, Robert Armstrong has bounced from job to job. They have often been long bounces. Armstrong is forty-eight years old and at times during his career he has flown jumbo jets on glamorous routes like New York–Europe. Once, flying a DC-8 into London, he watched as the contrails of other planes ahead of him knit a perfect web, pink in the blue dawn sky. "They pay us for this," his captain remarked in the silent cockpit, apropos of the heaven stretched in front of them. At other times Armstrong has made his living from scrap work, moving businessmen from one Georgia town to another in a lumpy single-engine plane he would repair with his own hands between flights. Armstrong is an artist. His employment status is no indication of his talent, any more than Picasso's might have been. People clear their throats when Robert flies, the way you might at a museum to silence the riff-raff around you. "There are only a few people in the world who can fly like that," Sergei Boriak says of Robert.

Armstrong has the Southerner's gift for universal laws laid down by the limits of his own experience, the mental geography of a man who only believes in the parts of the world he has seen with his own eyes. *Every Mexican restaurant in the state of Arkansas has ptomaine poisoning*, he will say assuredly. He follows the law with a story of woe and misery that features some beef fajitas.

Armstrong once worked for an airline called Legend, which operated out of Dallas in airplanes configured with only first-class seats. The company spent millions on a legal battle against American Airlines and millions on marketing, leaving it no money actually to run the airline. Thus Legend became history. Armstrong once worked for an Atlanta-based airline that specialized in toting rich people down to the Caribbean. It had trouble surviving the summers. Law: *The only people who run airlines are incompetent idiots.*

Once Armstrong was dating a girl who wanted to be a flight engineer. He helped her study for the F.E. test and then decided to take it for himself just out of curiosity. She scored 99 percent. He scored 19 percent lower. A job opened up. In those pre-ERA days the job went to the one with the mustache (the low scorer). Robert had a nice ride there, flying international legs on DC-8s. Before that job he had been as far west as Kansas and as far north as Oshkosh, Wisconsin, picking up airplanes. After a year on the DC-8 you could give him his passport and $500 and he'd go anywhere in the world. Including to a new job. At a startup. Which went under in a year. His girlfriend's 99 percent got her a job with a big airline, where she is now, twenty years later, a senior pilot with a regular check.

So maybe it isn't just the guys who run the airlines. It's not that Robert didn't want to work. He just had his mind elsewhere. Things always seemed to come easy enough, even when they came the hard way. Robert looked like a 1930s movie star, with a swashbuckler's mustache that was out of style everywhere except on his face. To tell the truth, he looked an awful lot like Ernest Hemingway, aged thirty-five. He was born and raised in Athens, Georgia. He was a natural with his hands, building everything from cars to planes. His father was a master at watch repair. Robert never went to college in Athens or anywhere else. *There is nothing to learn in college.* "I knew enough of the stuff that I lost interest," he says. His education was free, really. When he was in third grade, the Clark County Board of Education moved his school out to the Athens airport, back by the old hangars. Robert spent most of his time staring out the window. And what he saw led him to the runway at every recess. His mother had to come haul him away on Friday afternoons if she wanted to see him for dinner. Robert began washing planes in exchange for flying time. Throughout school he would change oil, fix tires, paint sun-chapped wings. Anything for free flight time. He flew all the way through his commercial certificates without ever paying for an hour of flight time. It was, and is, a catch-as-catch-can living.

Among the first things you find out when talking to Robert is how much everything costs. He sees this never ending financial commentary as one of the prerogatives of being broke. An hour of flight time costs $50. A crankshaft $7,500. Tires for the plane are $100. (Robert buys resurfaced ones for $28.) An overhaul for his eroding propeller costs $5,000, but Robert has a friend at the manufacturer who will do it for less. He's like a talking credit card bill. Or Andy Warhol. There is a weird quirk in Warhol's diaries that struck many people when they were first published in 1989. Warhol was *obsessed* with small expenditures. There he would be, hanging out with Mick and Jackie O. and worrying about the $2.50 cup of coffee or the $3.00 cab ride. "Went to White House today," he would write. "Wore new tie ($4.00)." Robert Armstrong is the Andy Warhol of aerobatics.

In December of 2000, Robert was west of Albuquerque flying an airliner to Las Vegas when a text message came onto a little display in the cockpit. It was from his bosses. The contents could be of little surprise to anyone who knew Robert. The airline would be going out of business at midnight. Law: *Every airline I work for goes under.* This worried Robert more than it might ordinarily. He was supposed to be a member of the 2001 U.S. National Aerobatic Team. He had won the spot by winning the U.S. Nationals in 1999. He had been counting on the regular airline paycheck to subsidize his practice for the World competition. When he made it home to Athens that weekend, he figured out exactly how much money he had in the bank. It was what some people might spend on a vacation. Then he counted out the number of days between December and the July competition. He figured out what it would cost per day to fly. He knew he should probably try to find another flying job. This had happened to him before, in 1996, out of work with a competition coming up. He became a master of the $2.49 taco special. He walked a few places instead of driving. Now he would again train instead of work. If need be he would train instead of eat.

Then he thought about what really mattered. The plane.

He needed a $40,000 engine. He didn't have $40,000. So he rummaged around his hangar, a warren so jammed with junk it could be a sitcom set, and found most of the parts. He built the engine himself ($4,000.) He had to buy insurance for the competition. ($1,800.) The Spaniards required it. So did the Commandments of Robert: *When you're nobody, and you show up at a contest, no one asks for your insurance. But if you show up and someone thinks you can beat them, you bet they'll be asking about insurance.* And this was the amazing thing, there was actually a shot, a very, very long shot in most eyes, that Robert Armstrong could go to Burgos, Spain, and win the World Aerobatic Championship. He would be competing against French and Russian pilots who were paid to train by their governments, against American teammates who had the latest equipment and the best coaching. He would be flying in a plane that was a decade past its prime. Robert Armstrong may sound like a pessimist, but like all the great pessimists, he is simply very carefully hiding away his real faith. "This is," the pessimist said one morning as he worked on a problem with his propeller, "a rich man's sport. I am just barely able to stay in it." Added the optimist: "Fortunately, the size of your wallet doesn't affect how you fly."

Plus, he had a secret. A living, breathing wallet. A benefactor. Like a Medici, a man with money who recognizes the power of art. If you drive up to the Athens airport on a weekend afternoon there is a damn good chance you will find Robert Armstrong's wallet sitting in the back of a pickup truck on a beat-up old lawn chair looking out over the runway. His wallet is named Brantley Coile. He is grading landings. "Eight point five," he'll say as a Beech Bonanza touches down, kicking a little left in a crosswind.

Brantley grew up here in Athens. And in 1990, following his tinker's heart, he left for Silicon Valley. Hated it there. But managed, in his Georgian way, to get to know everybody. So when he came home in 1992 to start a little consulting company, his phone kept ringing with calls from the coast. Men in trouble with machines who needed Brantley's help. *This mainframe won't start.* Brantley could give prescriptions over the phone. He became a long-distance pharmacist for sick machines. One day he got a call from a friend who was consulting for a *Fortune* 500 firm. The company had a problem. For starters, it had built an entire private computer network only to discover it couldn't communicate with the Internet.

To solve this problem, Brantley designed a machine that would translate the private network's mystifying internal corporate addresses into real-world computer addresses. Not only did this save the company the misery of having to reprogram every one of its machines, it made talking to the Internet safer and cheaper. Brantley's buddy suggested they put all this into a software program and sell it. But Brantley had seen enough of Silicon Valley to know that the only thing more fungible than software programmers were software programs. He wanted to build a box. Hardware.

It was a lotto decision, the kind of 1990s gut call that could transform a man into a multimillionaire. Brantley's little startup sold $3.5 million worth of boxes before it could get a sign on the door. Cisco Systems found it anyhow and brought a huge check. Brantley was now a very rich man. He continued to invent from Athens, later pioneering a program that lets companies use hundreds of computers at once to handle transactions on the World Wide Web. He has ten patents.

He has four airplanes. Flying back from California, Brantley made one of those little lists that people make when their lives are changing, a things-to-do-with-my-life list. One thing he wanted to do was succeed in business, to leverage what he'd done well so far. Another was to get into competition aerobatics. Flipping through *Flying* magazine, Brantley saw an ad for Shell Oil that had a picture of the 1992 U.S. Aerobatic Team. There, under a gruff-looking, mustachioed man standing next to a Pitts Special, were the words ROBERT ARMSTRONG. ATHENS, GEORGIA. Brantley thought: "He must be some stuck-up doctor or something."

Fridays at noon, life at the Athens airport slows. A flag hangs limp in the parking lot, tickled by a small breeze. Pilots wander in from all over the tarmac. Corporate guys pile out of their jets, pull at the back of their blue pants. From hangars around the field come private pilots, wiping oil from their hands, smelling the gas on their shirts. They pile into cars and make the quick drive to Clark's where they share barbecue and lemonade and stories. Some Fridays a half-dozen pilots make the pilgrimage. When there is Bulldog football, it can be nearly thirty.

Brantley began making the Friday lunches a habit. It took him weeks to figure out that Robert was there as well. He was still looking for his stuck-up doctor. Brantley tends to be quiet at times, while Robert fills every silence with a rainstorm. Ideas, opinions, stories. When the talk turned to aerobatics, Brantley put the puzzle together.

Robert was having a problem. His plane was simply out-classed at the world level. For the better part of a decade he had been competing against $200,000 factory-tuned planes in a ratty Pitts S1-C he had built himself. He was taking on aero-batic machines nicknamed ScreamingEagle and Thunder-Fury with a plane nicknamed "Road Kill." Oddly, he'd been winning, as if an old 1976 Volvo was killing Ferraris at For-mula One races. Nothing on that Pitts was normal. Robert had to remake the plane from the ground up, teaching himself engineering. Listening as much as he talked. But that would go only so far. The plane simply couldn't crank hard or fast enough anymore to be truly competitive.

After a few months of these stories, of Robert's never end-ing litany of costs and potential, Brantley decided it was time for him to buy Robert a plane he could win with. Together they flew down to Florida to look at an old CAP 231. It was so ugly that Robert said he was more likely to get sick looking at it than flying it. The gray and purple 231 was hardly state of the art. The entire French team were flying the latest version of the 23X series, a plane with a better wing and stronger engine. But Robert and Brantley felt this was their plane. Brantley wrote the $107,000 check. Robert flew the plane back to Athens.

. . .

Every man has a foundation myth about himself, a story that captures who he is. Or maybe the story just captures who he would like to be. Hemingway had his history as an ambulance driver in WWI, that youthful machismo like a moral I-beam as he constructed his life. For Napoleon it was the siege of Toulon. As a young officer he used artillery to drive the British out of the port city. He won a promotion to general and began his march to empire behind those cannons. Robert's foundation myth always had to do with scraping out wins as an underdog. But that was about to change. The CAP 231 gave him a new myth, a new sense of just how much he could do with his heart and hands.

Like any myth it began with a problem. Once he began flying the CAP, he scored fine, but when he pulled up vertical and began rolling he discovered the plane was slipping slightly off line. It was a tiny slide, but enough to change how the plane felt and how it looked in the air. Watching his flights on videotape, he saw the little bobble. One day, flying back from a competition, Robert noticed that he was holding left rudder just to keep the plane going straight. Even when he had everything perfectly centered, he could look out on the horizon as he flew through the flat spaces of Oklahoma and see the plane slowly peeling right. When he landed, he propped the plane up on supports to make sure the slip-and-bank indicator in the plane was dialed in correctly. It was. The puzzle stayed with him. Sometimes at night, Robert would sit and stare at the plane. *What can I make better?* One evening as

Robert was ogling his white-and-green repainted plane
($1,400) he noticed something strange. The engine was
slightly offset. It wasn't much, 6 degrees. You could fly a plane
for years without noticing. He called the factory the next day.
The French explained that it was offset intentionally. Several
of their engineers had insisted that the offset was required to
keep the plane stable. *Bullshit*, thought Robert. That tiny offset was what was keeping him from world-class performances.
It had to go.

Out came the welding gear. The tin shears. The new
pieces of metal. Working nights, he built a new, offset-free
engine mount. This is about the hardest thing you can do in
an airplane. It is a job for trained engineers. A mistake of a few
millimeters can cause the engine to rattle itself right off the
airplane. And in aerobatic flight, with the tremendous loads, if
it isn't built just right the mount can slip out of alignment.
When Robert called the CAP factory for advice you could
hear the French skepticism radiating across the Atlantic.
"Really," they insisted, "we know what we're doing. Leave the
offset." So he quit calling the factory. Once he rebuilt the
mount, he discovered the metal cowling that covered it was
now too small. So he reworked that as well. "Frankly, if I knew
it was going to be that big an ordeal . . . ," the pessimist
reflects. But with the engine straight, the CAP finally flew
right. The rolls were faster; the side-slip was gone. There was
no bobble as the plane climbed. The CAP handled like one of
the model planes Robert had flown as a kid. Sharp and true.
Whatever calculations that room full of French engineers had
made, they were wrong. Law: *All French engineers are idiots.*

Wandering around international competitions, Robert found a few CAP 231s on the flight line. Every one had a metal tab affixed to the left rudder to keep the plane flying straight. A kludge. And it still wasn't working: the offset would drag the planes sideways through the sky. What the hell kind of plane design was that?

Of course it wasn't just about the plane. No more than the story of Job was about the sheep. Robert Armstrong wasn't just rebuilding a plane, or simply coming up with new insults about the French. In his way, he was making a last-ditch attempt to hold on to the kind of aerobatics he loved, a sport where pilots built and flew their own planes. In the 1970s and 1980s, aerobatics flying was a bailing-wire-and-Scotch-tape kind of sport. During the week you built your plane. On the weekend you flew it. That was all changing. Robert dated it to the 1980s, to Wall Street's bull market. He remembered vividly, like a nightmare, a 1988 contest where a pilot arrived in a $40,000 Pitts Special he had paid someone else to build. The guy was so pumped up he taxied out to fly and had to come right back because he forgot his headset. Once he was finally in the air, this Donald Trump of the skies started a competition loop. It was huge. If he had had enough energy to finish it, it would have been 4,000 feet high. But he didn't. He stalled at the top. The airplane was on a bulletin board for sale a few weeks later. At the time $40,000 planes were astonishing to guys like Robert, an insane waste of money. A decade later you could hardly find a home-built plane at most Unlimited contests.

For some aerobatic pilots the charge of the sport is in the

risk of stepping over the line of the possible. Each flight has to be faster, harder, tougher than the last. Robert gets his joy from the limits of his plane, from knowing what it can do and performing right at those limits. He gets as much pleasure and gratification from working around a French engineering quirk as he does from flying well. He feels no need to go beyond what the plane can do.

"What kills people," he said one afternoon as the sun set outside the Athens airport, "is that they have a big ego, a bad attitude. A lot of people don't have any comprehension of what the mechanical limits of their planes are. One of the best Unlimited pilots recently had an elevator break," he said, referring to the surface that controls how the nose of the plane moves up or down. "Why? The plane had been repeatedly overstressed. You can do a snap roll as fast as you want, but there's a reason for the design limits. This guy was flying an airshow at Oshkosh and was starting his rolls coming down and when he finished the last point and pulled out, the airspeed needle had gone all the way around the meter and was showing about sixty knots *on the other side*. And he's still doing full deflection rolls. He's doing close to 300 knots. How many times can you abuse the equipment? You can do it once, twice. Maybe you can get away with it fifty times. But finally it broke. These guys push over the limits because someone said they should. I think some people think they can't do well unless they exceed the limits. Yeah I've put ten g's on the plane. But I never exceeded the design specs for the plane. I never had to. It doesn't have to be done. It's this attitude: 'I'm a doctor, I can do anything I want to. Here's my $250,000, I'm going to go win this contest.' There is a lot of that out there. And it doesn't do too well in the international arena."

The guys in Europe, the ones Robert respected, might be bankers and lawyers, but every one of them worked on their own planes. If something is rattling wrong, if the plane is slipping off line, they are the ones who reach for the tools, not some mechanic. If you want to be a great pilot, to have a chance at perfection, you have to know your machine. You can't subcontract that out, much as you may want to. The image of the great aerobatic pilot as a guy who just shows up and flies troubles Robert. If you are good, you must be working on your plane. "That quite possibly has a lot to do with the 'mystery' of flying," he says. "It's mechanical."

Darkness had settled on the field. Robert stretched his arms a bit. He had been up flying earlier, his first flight in nearly a month. A lack of money had kept him grounded most of the winter. Behind him, on the ramp, a few corporate jets were starting their engines. Robert's little grass-roots airport was getting busier these days with overflow jet traffic from Atlanta. He was still flying the way he was twenty years earlier when he first soloed a plane not 200 yards from where he was sitting now. He wandered back to his hangar to push the plane in for the night. All $107,000 of it—plus the years of work. Frankly, he wouldn't know what to do if you gave him a $250,000 plane and all the mechanical help he could use. The RoadKill II. It was just too bad the rest of the world wasn't playing by the same rules anymore.

The plane shudders with complaint.

The plane shudders with complaint. I am at 3,000 feet, flying snap rolls. I steady the plane at 110 knots. A deep breath in. Stick back quick. Then, fast as you read this, right rudder to the floor, hard as I can. The plane spirals around with a scream. It is screwing a hole in the sky, shaking and rattling as the wings stall and the propeller fights for a grip on the air. I feed the stick forward a bit, accelerating the roll, pushing for a more violent and punishing snap. The ground spins past below, the wing scoots backward on the horizon, an optical illusion. Almost level, I reverse the controls fast and then neutralize them, trying to catch myself after exactly a single rotation. I am off, 30 degrees maybe. My head clears and I go again: stick back, rudder in, hold on.

Misery radiates from the engine. I am covered in sweat from the work of controlling these snaps. They are essentially horizontal spins, though they have the instant violence of a car crash, the charmless horror of a knifing. A normal spin, where the plane falls earthward, takes a moment to work its way up to wild. It has a one or two rotation overture that is almost graceful, as the plane teeters over on its back and then sucks around into a full spin. It's not until the third or fourth rotation that the spin starts to accelerate like a spun top, whipping around with beautiful speed as the aerodynamics lock up the plane. The snap roll, which shoots straight ahead in the sky, is violent from the moment you touch the rudder.

As I come around level, I stop for a second and then push the plane hard through another couple of snap rolls. The wings bobble a bit. I'm pulling too hard, stalling the plane as I enter the figure. I find level, turn around, take a break. I lean my head back, stretching my neck, compressed by the g's. Seven positive, two negative according to the meter. All in less than a second. How to explain this again? The spins are as if Mishima had jumped from his balcony. Snap rolls are what really happened, the sudden blade on the back of his neck. "I can only think he went out of his mind," Prime Minster Eisaku Sato told the papers, his head bowed in confusion and shame.

I go again. Five in a row, like a revolver in a very poor game of Russian roulette. I finish disoriented and breathless, my pulse banging in my head, and the plane more off line than I would like. Five consecutive snaps are enough for me. I am working my way up to a dozen. When you get the rhythm right, you can bounce the snaps back to back like a ball against a wall. Pull-slam-pull-slam. Time becomes a loop, the growling of the plane makes a melody you cannot stop humming. Some Unlimited pilots take the rolls in consecutive dozens, a whole concert of violence. "The pilot," reads one National Transportation Safety Board report, "had been doing aerobatic snap rolls. After approximately 10–15 snaps he began another. As he pulled on the stick he 'felt the ailerons break loose.'" The ailerons turn the plane, a Russian Sukhoi-29. The appropriate reaction to having them break off is usually a curse, a fast grab for the canopy ejection level, and a prayer.

"The pilot recovered from the snap at 2,500 feet," the NTSB continued. "The airplane started a steep descending turn to the right. He attempted to right the airplane with back stick and left rudder to no avail. He elected to make a controlled landing in a turn." Here is what a *controlled landing* without ailerons looks like: "About 600 feet above the ground the wing went down to 90 degrees; the nose then went down till impact with the ground. At no time did he have any directional or aileron control of the airplane."

The engineers at the NTSB found a hairline crack in the Sukhoi, an erosion in the straw-sized wire that tied the cockpit controls to the wings. The stress of the repeated snaps was wearing away at that system like the sun on ice. The problem was so deeply buried that nothing short of a microscope would have revealed it in a preflight inspection. It was a time bomb. The Sukhoi had no history of these fractures. The pilot survived the crash.

I am straight and level again, coming around in a hard bank, setting up for another snap. I pull to 45 degrees nose up. Stop there. Brace myself. Snap again. The rolls are more difficult on an upline like this since I don't have the ground below for reference. The engine screams from the load on the propeller. Does everything feel normal? Even though I am trying to relax through these figures, I am alert to signs of problems with the plane. There is the idea in most motor sports that greatness involves a marriage of man and machine. It is a strange marriage up here, as if I have wed a nymphomaniac. I am on constant prowl for signs of danger. Is that a piece of wire on your collar?

Our dealings must be as respectful as they are joyous. We must have the delicate interaction that you might expect in a long marriage. We might ask ourselves quietly, at night, maybe after a strained dinner: Who is going to snap first?

For the longest time it was the planes. Until a couple of decades ago, the best planes could hold together through six g's before things would start to shred away. So the sport became contained by those physical limits, a kind of notional box, its sides made up of every nightmarish airshow mistake we had seen: a pilot pulling hard to avoid the ground, shedding wings and gear and engine like a peeling banana. The sudden stopping of the engine sound. The loud report. Its parameters were easy to remember, even if you slipped outside them from time to time. Six g positive; two negative. Inside that envelope you could try wonderful things. Outside, the flying was suicidal.

Then, in the 1970s, the Soviets started experimenting with composite airframes that were light enough to fly hard maneuvers and strong enough to withstand them. It took a while to learn to fly these new machines. The areodynamics were tricky, sure. But what was hardest was learning to accept that the plane could go wherever your mind wanted. Eventually, however, these single-wing stilettos began displacing the little biplanes that had dominated the sport for a couple of decades. It was possible to do things in them—turn aerial corners at ten g's for instance—that pilots had only dreamed of before. The new planes wound what was once an aerial ballet into something more like karate or disco dancing. The ballet had left town, actually. And the circus had arrived.

. . .

Every great aerobatic design begins like a symphony, with a single idea for a melodic line. Classical aerobatics of the 1930s were Chopin-like, proud of regular rhythms, ennobled by stately harmonies. Thus the aircraft. They were called things that sounded like the names of continental debutantes: the high-winged Morane-Saulnier, the speedy Dewtoitine. You could take them out and dance, but they had to be home early. Papa was waiting. "Go out there and *fuck them with that plane*," Sergei shouted at Kirby Chambliss as he harnessed himself into an Edge 540 before his last flight in the 1998 World Championships. You would have never heard language like that about a Bucher-Jungmeister.

The earliest aerobatic pilots were near direct descendants of the gentlemen aviators who pioneered flying itself. These were the men who gathered cheerfully in London in 1914 for an "Upside Down Dinner." Requirement for invitation: you must have been inverted in an airplane, rare enough at that time. White or black tie was the dress code. Dinner was served "inverted," starting with coffee and dessert and working on to soup. A Blierot monoplane was hung upside down over the tables. When Bentfield Hucks, the first Briton to have looped a plane, opened the evening with an "after-dinner" speech he began with "And finally" and concluded with "Good evening." The white ties around the table harrumphed approvingly.

None of this for Leo Loudenslager, thanks. The smash-mouth aerobatics he and his peers made up forty years later were as pure 1960s and '70s as the Pucci dress or the Beetle.

Great pilots see their flying as a mirror. How we fly reflects something about us, and a bit of our times too. The gentlemen aviators of the 1920s knew that. So did those who came after them. In the late 1960s, for instance, the Czech pilots who began using the propeller force of their new Zlins to tumble through the sky were university-educated men, charming and literate relics from an older Czech Republic. They had a memory of life before Soviet times. They could recite poetry. The street names in Prague celebrated men like Masaryk. So was it a surprise when these pilots found expression and relief even in a violent figure like the Lomcovak? Maneuvers like that demanded a spirit of improvisation, a passion for disharmony, an ability to translate an excited pulse into delirious flight. Everything that was banned in the Soviet Union was stuffed into that one idea of what to do with a plane. If aerobatics was a blend of man and machine it required a certain kind of man, a certain moment in his life. And, of course, it required a certain kind of very fine machine.

The kind of flying Walter Extra had in mind—violent, kinky stuff—would have flabbergasted the people who knew him in Cologne as the family man who smilingly blitzed through Chopin on his piano. "Walter?" they might ask searchingly if you told them about his flying habits. "The nice man who rides dressage? The one with the perfect horses with the braided tails?" They wouldn't have believed what Walter liked to do in a plane. It was like learning your priest had a leather habit. Extra looked a bit like a Lutheran preacher. He had the same patient eyes, the easy smile, the aura of listening to you even while he was talking. But there was something happening behind those eyes.

You could ask him what the appeal of aerobatics was. He would say at least that he had taken to it almost as soon as he started flying in the 1970s. But he still couldn't really say what the attraction was, just that sense of wanting to do something different in the air. He would stare for a while, quietly grinning, honestly perplexed. It was like asking Don Juan why he liked women. Extra quickly became one of the best German pilots. Then among the best in Europe and, shortly, among the best in the world. What marked his flying was a kind of constrained chaotic rigor, like something from a supercomputer model of a nuclear explosion. It was complex, beautiful, clearly dangerous flying. It was expert, though. You might take a figure like an outside three-quarter loop with a half-snap on the top. That was the kind of figure that could bring out the worst in a pilot: impatience, or an understandable greed to get away from the negative g's. But Extra was so interested in containing the figure, in flying it as a tight little shape, that the temporal worries, the physical pain faded. He had stability in his life with the Chopin, the horses. He didn't need it in the air.

So here was a problem that bothered him. Imagine pulling from horizontal flight to straight-up vertical. It's impossible, of course, to make that turn as a sharp corner. You can't stop the plane in midair, turn the nose up, and then keep flying. What the pilot really manages is something akin to a quarter of a loop. But as planes became stronger, the radius of that turn, the transition from flat to vertical, got tighter. The turn became *the* test of a new plane. How hard could you go around the corner before something snapped? Could you make an aerodynamic design that didn't stall as the g's got higher? Walter wanted square corners, even if they meant putting ten positive or ten negative g's on the plane. His sky music demanded a machine that would climb like a rocket, roll like a yo-yo, and stop in midair as if it had hit a wall. And corner like a miter saw. Not to stretch a point, but he wanted to do for flying what Rommel had done for tank warfare. He wanted to make it fast, violent, and decisive. To do that he needed a Panzer of the air, something as tough as it was fast.

It couldn't be figured out on a computer. You might think that after nearly a century of flight the physics were knowable. Wasn't there a German in some lab somewhere like Stuttgart who could just punch in the numbers and get an answer: make the wing this long, do such and such with the tail? Perhaps the NASA guys? No, they were the ones who kept an aerobatic Pitts two-seater at their test-pilot training school and wouldn't let anyone solo in it. Amid a fleet of fifty planes, everything from 737s to F-16s, it was the one plane the test-flight guys weren't allowed to fly alone. Imagine, a fighter jock just off a carrier, hottest stick in his squadron, being forced to have a ride-along, like some sixteen-year-old kid trying to get a driver's license. But that was the deal. There were simply too many variables once you started breaking away from straight and level flight. It made the design of air-planes more art than science.

This was the reason guys like Walter Extra could build

world-class planes. Of course he needed to keep the engineering laws in mind, needed to have a sense of stresses and strains. Several generations of dead pilots had proven that. But great design also demanded a sense of artistry. And that was rare. You couldn't get it at M.I.T. Curtis Pitts, father of the great American biplane of the 1970s never went to college. He was a self-taught engineer. But he had the gift, what Napoleon called the *coup d'oeil*, the skill of great generals to see all of a battlefield in a single glance. Pitts could see what was right and wrong in a plane design with a single look. Even when he was ninety years old, living in Homestead, Florida, Pitts still designed planes with a protractor. And solved problems that perplexed younger designers, men with big computers behind them.

Pitts had lost most of his fire by that time, had it extinguished by the years of lawsuits that were like bad jokes. Heard this one? "Guy walks into a propeller . . ." And sues Curtis. The juries looked to Pitts for money, driving him out of the business. He went on designing, though, doing it the old way. The highest-tech thing in his shop was the trap he had rigged up by the door in case a burglar snuck in on him while he worked. It consisted of a cocked pistol and ten feet of twine tied to the doorknob.

Aerobatics involved a number of mysteries that weren't easy to solve. It wasn't until the 1980s, for instance, that engineers began to understand why airplanes spun—a problem that had been around since the Wright brothers. The spin begins when the plane quits flying. The engine is still running strong, but if the pilot brings the stick far enough back it's possible to scoot the wings so far up that they stop generating lift from the air passing over them. Imagine sticking your hand outside the window of a speeding car. You hold it level into the air stream and by twisting it back and forth you can make it go up or down. But twist your hand to 70 or 80 degrees. Instead of flying, it sinks into the passing air. This is what happens when the wing on a plane stalls: its angle can no longer generate lift, no matter how fast you are going. So the wing falls, and the plane feels as if it is dropping away like a leaf. Generally this is easily recoverable. Push the nose of the plane down and the wing picks up the airflow and begins flying again. In aerobatic lingo, the airflow has "reattached" to the wing.

But if you keep the wing stalled, as the plane begins to slip down into the sky like a car on ice, you can enter a spin by jamming down on the rudder, skewing the plane to the side. One wing accelerates ahead of the other as you do this. Think of your right hand as a wing with a little pivot in the palm. If you hold the hand level and turn it to the left side you'll see that the pinky finger moves quickly forward while the thumb pivots nearly in place. The same thing happens on a spin entry. The rudder kick speeds up the right wing relative to the left. That excess speed on the right side creates an imbalance in lift and sends the plane skidding over onto its back, right wing high, and into a spin.

This terrified early pilots; then it killed them. The natural reaction—pulling hard back on the stick to stop the plane from screaming earthward—is wrong. A hard pull causes the rotation rate to accelerate. Hundreds of pilots have sailed to their deaths in just this ignorant pose, furiously pulling back on their control sticks in an effort to get the plane back up. Nose high, they smash into the ground, still stalled.

This solution to the spin problem was discovered by the pilots themselves, not the airplane designers. It was first detected when pilots began bailing out of spinning airplanes during the 1920s. Often they noticed that as soon as they had jumped out, the planes stopped spinning and settled into a dive. The machines would recover and teeter through the sky until finally running out of gas and crashing, miles away from the mortified pilots. With these examples in mind, some pilots began to notice that planes corrected almost as soon as they climbed out of the cockpit to jump. It is 1924 and you have just spun your mailplane. Certain you will not survive a landing, you let go of the stick, unstrap from the plane, and begin climbing over the side. *I hope this chute works.* And, just as you are about to jump, you notice: the plane is flying again. You climb gingerly back into the cockpit. One foot. Then another. *Is it going to spin again?* you wonder. But it doesn't. It stays stable. You fly off and land, very confused.

The key, it turns out, was that moment when you gave it all up, when you let go of the stick and started climbing sadly out of the plane. Left to their own devices, without your inputs, the controls naturally centered themselves in the air-flow. The nose dropped down a bit and the wings started fly-ing again. If you stayed in the cockpit you could stop an incipient spin in exactly the same way. Thus was born the ear-liest spin-recovery technique: hands-off, power-off, wait. In the 1970s the technique was refined by two pilots, Erich

Müller and Gene Beggs, into the technique that is now taught as a standard last-ditch procedure for aerobatic pilots. Hands off the controls, chop the power, and push on whichever rudder feels heavier. You have centered the controls. Wait. Sit there for a few rotations, the ground coming up at you, doing nothing and waiting for the spin to turn into a dive. Not recovered yet? Keep waiting. You don't have to know much about pilots to know how hard it is to get us to do so little, even to save our lives.

Müller-Beggs works, but it is sloppy as hell. It is an emergency technique. The plane will recover, but you cannot predict when. Competition aerobatics demands a precise spin entry and recovery. *Not only can I survive the spin*, your flying must say, *but I will then wantonly head straight down as fast as I can.* A great spin is always in control. A great aerobatic flight is a testament to controlling the uncontrollable.

This was the kind of flying Extra wanted to engineer. Most of the pre-1980s-era planes were too loose for real accuracy in the air. They were controlled, for instance, with wire cable-and-pulley systems made from wound-up lengths of steel wire. But the wires wiggled so much that a pilot could stand at the tail and hold the elevator in place while a friend poked the stick from side to side in the cockpit. The wings of the planes, designed for strength, were often overengineered: heavy and pocked with drag-inducing rivets. There were other problems too, like control imbalances which meant that you needed different amounts of force to turn the plane or make it climb. And sometimes terrible design errors. Not enough internal bracing in the wings. Too few guy-wires to hold the tail on. Weak landing gear. They were the kind of flaws you found out about only when they killed someone. A little flu of these lessons broke out in Europe in the early 1980s, planes coming apart in midair. Pilots rarely survived.

Extra built a machine to fix these problems. He connected the stick to the control surfaces with steel rods, eliminating the looseness. If you held on to the tail of an Extra, you couldn't move the stick at all. In the air, the Extra was so sensitive it seemed to read your mind, it seemed to hear every sick Teutonic perversity you might have there. The tiniest bit of pressure on the stick bumped the plane off equilibrium and into a climbing or turning or descending dance. Extra's plane was among the first to reliably clock roll-rates greater than 360 degrees a second. It could climb thousands of feet straight up while still maintaining enough energy to roll and snap. Straight down it was a beast. Shaped from smooth composite fiber, the plane's clean wings had no structural junk popped sluggishly into the airstream. Nose over in the plane, pour gas in the engine, and you could see nearly 300 miles an hour in less than ten seconds.

And it would never break. Extra had eliminated—he hoped—the problem of planes shattering in flight by bolting those composite wings onto a welded steel frame. On racks at his factory, the wings had been stressed to twenty times the force of gravity. Once some workers took that up to thirty times. The wings groaned, but they did not break. Extras had crashed, but they were so well made that there were none of the stories of planes shedding their wings in midair that haunted other types. In 1996, Rick Masagee, one of the best American aerobatic pilots, bought a new Sukhoi 31 made with composite wings in Russia. He had it shipped to Florida and painstakingly inspected and rebuilt. Every detail was checked and rechecked. On his first flight Masagee pulled hard to vertical and snapped both wings clean off the plane, as if he'd broken a cocktail stick. Masagee's family and friends watched as the wingless plane murdered him into the ground. The carbon-fiber wing spar, an I-beam-like piece that holds the wings in place, was cracked and as weak as glass. An impossible problem to detect. "Epoxy, vodka. Epoxy, vodka," was how a friend described the Russian composite-curing system at the time.

For Extra pilots, the German engineering mythos was like a reassuring back rub every time the plane started to rock and hiccup. When pilots got in trouble in an Extra it was because the plane was better than they were: too fast, too slick, too easy to cast into wild gyrations. This was plenty of trouble, though, enough to kill the best pilots even with the wings still attached. The plane was strong enough to get you out of trouble, but fast enough to get you in it before you could adjust. Take Ken Hadden, an aerobatics inspector pilot who bought an Extra 200 back in 1997. Fifty years old with several thousand hours of flying time in his logbooks. He was sharp enough that the government had designated him an Aerobatic Check Examiner, certified to give out the rare permits that allow ground-level aerobatics in front of crowds. He was a former U.S. National Glider Aerobatics champion. Hadden landed at a small grass strip to show his friends his plane. Filled up with gas. Took off for home. *See you later, guys.* Just after lifting off the runway he pulled up smartly to 45 degrees nose high and performed a half-roll to inverted. This left him upside down about 500 feet off the runway. He then began to pull back on the stick to bring the plane arcing down through the air. It was a beautiful thing to watch. The plane handled it marvellously, picking up speed. Extra himself couldn't have flown it better. But he probably would have flown it higher. The problem with a loop like this is that you have no sense of how far above the ground you are until you are about to, well, run into it. So Hadden had this fantastic view of the earth but almost no idea how far up he was until he smashed into the ground, killing himself. It was a shame. He really loved that plane. It couldn't have cared less about him.

Sometimes
a man can become possessed
by a vision.

Sometimes a man can become possessed by a vision. Perhaps it makes no sense to anyone else; perhaps it is a revelation to everyone. Yes, this man will say to himself, this is the way the world is supposed to be. This is how I am supposed to fit into it. He will know, like a man trying on shoes, that he has finally found a pair that will serve him for a very long walk indeed. So he begins, one step at a time. I am going to tell you, in a moment, a story about aerobatics. I don't want you to mistake it for a pilot's story. I will come later to the grand themes, which involve the faith men have in themselves and the reasons we keep that faith. One excellent example of those themes, however, would be John Coltrane. February 1959. The Sutherland Hotel, New York. The jazz pianist Warren Bernhardt wandered by to eavesdrop on 'Trane and Miles Davis at work. "Coltrane was playing 45-minute solos in those days," Bernhardt recalled later. "He would never take the horn out of his mouth. Then, all through the breaks, there was a couch near the bar that went into the kitchen and Coltrane would lie down on the couch with his feet up and practice real quietly you know, it was just like this whisper. You'd go to the men's room and walk by him and hear lots of scales and stuff."

Coltrane had a problem in his head, and he was trying to

work it out the way you or I might do our checking account sums. Inspiration would make a deposit, a Dorian chordal line for instance, thick, resplendent, scented like a souk. And Coltrane would draw down that balance like a miser, one note at a time, for years, as he worked to make his sound. It was no different, really, than Gaudi and his cathedral or Picasso making Guernica or James writing *The Golden Bowl*. Each man was given a vision of reality, a biblical and sudden vision. Then, just barely, handed what he needed to make the vision real. The strength came hissing out of these great men in little bits. A whisper. "Genius does what it must," the old saw goes. "Talent what it can." These men could only do one thing. They could only try to carve the world into accordance with their reality. What kind of maniac plays a forty-five-minute saxophone solo and then sits down and keeps playing quietly to himself? Is there any task more pure? Any task greater?

It is not the case, as F. Scott Fitzgerald said, that genius is the ability to hold two diametrically opposed ideas in your head at one time and still retain the ability to function. I suppose that is some kind of genius, but I can't imagine what it produces. No, we're working closer here to Emerson's line, the one that defines genius as "believing that what is true in your heart is true in the hearts of all men." This is just the start. Greatness is not only about belief, but still more about action. You have an idea that you think is correct. Perhaps everyone disagrees. No one understands what you are after. But you follow that vision, even when there are lots of reasons for doing the wrong thing, the easy thing. Like I said, this is not a story about aerobatics. It is a story about will and motion.

. . .

They withheld secrets from him. Not that this was a crime. You might have done the same. Your national pride, your company, your vision on the line. But there was no arguing they hid the secrets. Little things, sure, like how to tune the wings so the rolls in the air would stop and start crisply, as if the plane were smacking something solid. Big things, like what the plane could really handle before it would crumble in midair and disintegrate, taking the pilot with it for a final, screaming ride. I mention these here to give you a sense of the obstacles a man can face. He knew what he wanted to do. And in making his vision real, he faced not only the challenges of carving it from the ether of his mind, but of building it amid the bullshit of other people. They didn't tell him about adjusting the ailerons. He didn't care.

In 1977 David Martin saw Leo Loudenslager fly. Martin was eighteen, prime west Texas beef. Big, grinning, young, stupid, all the good stuff. He spent most of his days out on the west Texas lakes where he was raised. The Possum Kingdom they called it, once a home to the largest pseudo-fur industry in the United States. On a good Friday night, locals recalled in half-jest, you could go out with a six-pack of beer, a pickup truck, and a box of .22 ammo and kill an evening picking off possums as they wandered stupidly through your headlights. In the morning you'd wake up hungover in the back of your truck cab and the little possum bodies would be shotgunned out across the mesa like some story from World War II. The lone private in his foxhole. The machine gun. The mounds of

Jap bodies at dawn. In the 1960s the Possum Kingdom was a
training ground for American chopper pilots. Those boys
couldn't get enough of the possum game, blowing off steam
before heading to Vietnam. That was David Martin's world.
But when he was eighteen he saw something a little farther
out than the range of those headlights. He heard a whisper. It
happens to some people. A plane overhead, they wonder
where it is headed. David saw Leo Loudenslager flying. He
wondered what it would be like to be like that. He became
afflicted with a vision of flying like Leo. The world suddenly
looked much bigger than west Texas.

To begin with he wanted a plane *just like Leo's*. There was
only one way to get such a plane: build it. He could have
bought another plane, abandoned the vision. But David
wanted to fly *just like Leo*. It took him fourteen years to finish
the plane. He befriended Leo in the process. When Leo put
the notice in *Sport Aerobatics* asking people to please quit calling him for advice—*it was getting in the way of the flying*—
David Martin wasn't one of the people he meant. Leo always
had time for him. The project to build a Laser plane like Leo's
followed David everywhere. It came with him to college, to
military training camps. He would drag it along with him in a
trailer and use his spare time to weld wings together, to fiddle
with the canopy seals. When David finally finished his Laser
in 1992 he began training to make the U.S. Unlimited Aerobatics team. He had never flown in an Unlimited aerobatic
contest in his life. His wife Martha, the blond and perfect
dream of every Texas schoolboy, watched him from the
ground. Taught herself how to judge aerobatics so she could

help David fly better. (She didn't care much for the flying her-self.) David would fly every day. Martha would drive out and set under him, walkie-talking reassurance. "That looked good, honey," she would say, holding the radio in her per-fectly manicured fingers. Neither one of them really knew what they were looking for. David came home every night darkly worried. He spent an entire year flying the Unlimited known sequence, the set program of figures that pilots use for their first competition flight, over and over again, like practic-ing the same five measures of Schubert. Except that if you missed a note you would find yourself at 500 feet trying to catch an inverted spin before it wrapped itself up, your wife watching the whole time. Keep the plane in control, he said to himself that year. Just fly the plane. That is enough. Leo hadn't designed his plane for stability. Shit, he hadn't designed it for anyone but himself.

In September 1992, David Martin arrived at U.S. Nation-als in his plane. He had seen quite a few Nationals before. He'd even imagined flying in them. In 1980, when the United States hosted the World contest for the first time, he day-dreamed about scrapping the Laser, buying a Pitts, and trying to rush onto the team. But, *he wanted to fly just like Leo.* So he stuck with the plan. Sometimes he'd see if he could get his regular flying to be Leo-sharp. He'd come home from a long day beating an F-16 around the sky with his Texas Air National Guard buddies and climb right into the open cockpit of his 1936 Bucker-Jungmeister. He'd circle idly over the Pos-sum Kingdom airport quietly snapping the old plane as the sun set.

So he shows up in Dennison, Texas, and proceeds to fly one of the best 1977-style performances at the competition. In fact, it's safe to say it is the best 1977-style performance. Unfortunately for David Martin, it is 1992. He had taken too long to build his plane. He wasn't well enough trained. Fourteenth place. He watched the top Unlimited pilots flying and picked up that smell of a different species. He watched them beat him. How could he become like that? Better than that? "Dream is gone," he told Martha. *I am going to build a Laser like Leo and win the National Championship.* Gone. "Gotta do something different," he told Martha.

So David Martin bought a new plane, an Extra 300S. He hated it at first. Couldn't get it to snap roll properly. Had a tough time holding lines. Maybe what they said about the Extra, that it couldn't be snapped well, was true. Maybe it wasn't the plane for him. A week before 1993 Nationals, the new Extra arrived in the Possum Kingdom. Martin loaded it up and took off for Dennison to at least watch Nationals, to study the other sculptors at work, to pick up their tricks. He wasn't ready to fly himself and didn't know if he ever would be. But, would you believe it, right at the competition, he had another vision: Sergei Boriak, new to the United States, flying. Martin was still puzzling over his Extra as he sat in the stands, still thinking maybe the plane couldn't snap. Then he saw Boriak exploding in the sky in *his* Extra. Actually, it wasn't Boriak's plane. He didn't have two rubles to rub together and was mowing lawns to make ends meet. But Walter Extra had loaned Boriak the plane so he could show the world what it could do. And what couldn't it do! Geez. The Kazakh's snap rolls hardly moved from side to side in the sky. Boriak won the first flight. He won the second flight. When the time came to fly the last flight he drew the first slot, a notoriously impossible position since judges score low early on to leave room to reward other pilots. Some whispered the positioning was a conspiracy to make sure a foreigner didn't win the U.S. championship. Boriak didn't care. He finished second overall. "That's what I want to fly like," David Martin said to himself.

"Explain to me aerodynamics of snap roll," Boriak said to him on their first day together. "Wrong," Sergei spit into the middle of Martin's mumbled reply. You were always wrong with Sergei, even when you were right. He had his own Soviet-issue explanation for everything. But if you listened, his Commie explanations were capable of transforming you from the pilot you were into the man you wanted to be. It was as if there were a dead-bolted door between the room you lived in and the one you wanted to inhabit. Sergei was the key.

Boriak will tell you that Martin doesn't have as much raw talent as some pilots he's seen. Boriak will tell you that at Martin's house. He'll tell you that *in front* of Martin. But at their level of competition it's not about raw talent. It's about the refined stuff. Stick skills buffed and polished by groaning, sweaty cockpit hours and a kind of mental hardness that can break a man's heart. Only a dozen or so people on the planet have as much of the refined stuff as Martin. In 1994 he flew 225 hours of aerobatics practice, about as much as you can possibly fly in a year. He would get up in the mornings, drive to the airport, check out the plane, fly five minutes to his practice area, and exhaust himself. He would do that three or four times a day. Five, six hundred training flights in a year. It was awful at times. "If you are having fun practicing," Martin would say to himself as his plane bounced out to the practice area yet again, "you are not practicing hard enough." Sometimes after he landed Martin would sit quietly in his cockpit listening to the engine ticking and the sound of a west Texas night coming down. He'd start to feel chill in his shirt. He'd pop open the canopy to let some fresh air blow in. He sit there for a moment thinking about everything he had to learn. It seemed immense. Deep breath. *Like Leo.*

The unknowns were just killing him. Anyone could come to a contest and crank their way through a known, something they had been practicing for a year. So the contests also included two unknown flights, programs delivered to the pilots just twenty-four hours before they were to be flown. Each country submitted a different figure to the international jury. The jury picked ten or so that worked well together and then the teams labored to produce a sequence that used all ten. Those complete sequences were passed back to the judges who vetted them for safety, then selected one and distributed it to the pilots. No practice flights allowed.

It was really impossible to prepare for this sort of challenge. You could try to mind-fly your way through the sequences, and good pilots did that. On hotel-room floors at the Worlds, you'd find a taped-out square marked just like an aerobatic box, maybe three feet by three feet. At night, their flights twitching ahead of them like a scheduled biopsy, the pilots would stand in the boxes and shuffle through the sequences. To simulate an upline they might bend backward. Forward for a downline. Twisting left and right as the plane would do. But even if you could memorize the sequence of figures before you took off, saving you the trouble of consulting the little Aresti notation card taped into the cockpit, what you saw in the air was strange, dangerous. You could practice unknown maneuvers every day, but that was like trying to train for an argument with your wife. Nothing went as planned. Guys like David Martin could fly snap rolls on a descending 45-degree line every day of the week. But in competition they needed to be able to make them look sharp at the wrong speed or the wrong altitude or both. More than one pilot has plowed into an unknown sequence and found himself, halfway through, loading up for a maneuver he half-suspected would end at the ground. But you needed to be ready to press the figures out at any altitude, in any order. There were times you couldn't see what you were doing. Flying straight up in the air, for instance, there were no outside references. All you could see was sky. But you still had to move the plane precisely. In fact, if you tried to look outside the plane to line yourself up on something like the clouds or the sun, you would screw up.

The only way to master unknowns was to have total control of your plane, your flying, and your mind. Then, maybe, you would have a chance. In the early days of competition it was considered a success to get through an unknown sequence without a zero, without flubbing a figure entirely. In the 1980s that had changed. It was possible, just possible, to finish an unknown and score well. But by the late '90s zeros were back like rain. The figures were so hard, the maneuvers so extreme, that simply finishing the flight had become, again, enough.

The nerves too had to be mastered. They surprised Martin. Even after three, four years of flying he'd go to set up for a competition spin and find his right leg hammering away like a sewing machine against the rudder. As a kid Martin used to wax ass on the lakes near his home as a competitive water skier. Heart cold as the water. His brother would be outside coughing up a lung with nerves and David would be happily flipping through a magazine or chatting up a girl or fiddling with his skis. *My brother was always nervous and that was his weak point.* But nerves were now a weak point for David. Flying changed you, good and bad. He wasn't alone. One friend of Martin's, a national champion, told David how he stood in alone in the crappy little white-tile bathroom at the Dennison, Texas, airport just quaking—even his fingers shook—before his championship flight. "*Before* he got in the airplane," Martin marveled later. That was the kind of pressure he dreamed of: one flight to win the national championship. To win a world championship.

Martin first made the U.S national Unlimited team in 1998. They say it takes five to seven years for a talented pilot to become a world-class Unlimited competitor. There are exceptions like young Alan Bush, for instance, or Xavier L'Apperant, world champion at twenty-four. But that frame had been about right for David, who hit his early forties and his competitive pace in the late 1990s. He had nailed some good finishes at U.S. Nationals: second place once, fourth twice. He was still struggling with parts of his flying even as he won, fighting to make the plane look *just like Leo.* David wanted to become the first American world champion since Leo in 1980. And he began to sense that for all its strength and smooth design, the Extra simply wasn't sharp enough. He changed planes again. This wasn't an easy choice. Switching planes isn't like hopping in a new car. Learning to fly a new plane can mean a setback of years before you get back to the precision you had in your old plane. Even the differences between individual planes of the same design could be extreme. Flying someone else's Extra, for instance, David might look 10 or 20 percent worse. So swapping the Extra for a whole new plane was a risk.

But when David bought a French CAP 232 in 1998, the French sort of forgot to pass along a few details. For starters, their designers had subtly changed the roll-enhancing aileron spades on the plane they gave him. The spades hung under the wing and helped the ailerons catch the air in a turn. The change wasn't much, the new ones were just slightly bigger. But David could tell his plane wasn't behaving in the same way as the ones he was watching the French team win with. "Is there some difference?" he politely asked his friends at the CAP factory in Lyons. Blank stares. Smiles. *"Non,* the plane is fine." At the world contest in 1998, Martin paced around the French 232s and noticed that they *were* subtly different, particularly in the configuration of the ailerons on the wings. David's plane, for instance, had come with a little bit of tape covering the space between the ailerons and the wing itself.

This was a tiny gap, maybe half an inch. The tape was supposed to stop air from sneaking through the opening, it was
supposed to present a more solid wing, one that stopped
faster. But as Martin strolled quietly among the French team
planes at the '98 World contest—hands in pocket, just a kid,
gosh, looking innocently at these neato planes!—he noticed
something: no tape. At the 2000 World Championships he
watched perplexed as a mediocre British pilot blazed a flight
in a CAP he had bought directly from Patrick Paris, the 1998
French world champion. Martin grilled the man: the plane
was *not* like his. The spades had a different shape. The aileron
controls hung differently. "Oh, yes, we forgot to mention
that," the French said when Martin asked later. G-loads?
Never put more than nine on the plane, the factory warned. It
would burst like a bunch of toothpicks. In 1999 Martin put
ten and a half on a plane during a flight. Called the factory.
Nervous as hell. Had he just turned a $250,000 plane into a
pile of scrap? "Just reset the meter," they said. *Tant pis.*

The French were playing for keeps. They were happy to
sell their planes abroad but they were fucked if they were
going to give away their secrets. Since 1980 the big aerobatics
training machines in Russia and France had only gotten more
powerful: bigger budgets, more government attention. The
French team was fighting hard just to keep the Russians at
bay. They didn't need a revamped American team to compete
with as well. *Let them buy the planes,* the thinking went. *But we
must still win.*

The French team was a little island of Gallic talent and
snobbery. It was largely staffed by French military pilots

assigned to competition duty. Team coaches would choose the best pilots from the whole of the L'Armee de l'Air, give them new shoulder patches, train them every day. The government paid for the latest planes, hired ace mechanics to keep them in perfect working order, let engineers tweak the ailerons and goose the motors. So the planes were perfect. And replaceable. Go ahead and break it, the coaches would say in practice, we'll get you another from the hangar. Heh, heh. They knew the joke, knew the government would play along so long as they won. At their little training camp down in Marseilles, after a hard day of flying, they would all wander off to the local yoga studio together, and then out to a night of flying stories over red Bordeaux and brie. Was foie gras part of the training regimen this year? The French coaches seemed to vet their pilots for looks as much as skill. *But Pierre, will he look good in the jumpsuit?* Of course he would. They all did. Patrick Paris, the 1998 world champion, was fifty years old, almost as bald as a cue ball, and still looked like a male model. Glistening blue eyes, Gallic grin, flew like he was running through St. Germain de Pres with Bardot, a Gauloise on his lips. How the hell do you beat that if you're a guy from west Texas, a guy who grew up thinking a cultured Friday night involved Budweiser and an unlimited supply of possum?

Eddy Dussau, for instance. Eddy was the great hope of the French aerobatic team in 2001. Martin came to the 2001 games in his best form ever, just off a second place finish at the U.S. Nationals. He had trained harder than any other American pilot for the Worlds. But he was up against the likes of Eddy. The whole contest site was plastered with his picture.

Eddy, not yet thirty, *four-time* French national champion, talking to kids. Eddy getting out of his plane. Eddy training. Or, best of all, the poster: Eddy on a 45-degree upline, French sky behind him, grinning away from behind features so sharp that it seemed he could, in the event of an emergency, cut his way out of the cockpit with his nose. The way Eddy flew his fire-engine-red plane made you realize this wasn't just about looks. He flew impossibly hard, tight sequences. His specialty was the way he started maneuvers. "It is about how you begin," Coco Bessier, the team coach, explained. Eddy started his maneuvers the way the French probably wished they had defended the Maginot line. Fast, angry, desperate. There was a downside to this: no room for error. Dussau flew with 100-percent commitment, slamming from figure to figure as fast as possible. It was a beautiful style. It gave him almost no time to adjust his speed, position, or entry between figures. If Eddy flew well he'd win the Worlds in a walk. If he made even a tiny mistake, however, there would be no time to recover before it was written out on the sky. But, even losing, he would still be the prettiest at the competition, *non?*

Maybe the Russians had a similar looks-based system? Except they chose the ugliest pilots. It fit their brutal kind of flying. They ran their camps like tractor factories. Thirty hard days of camp a year at Borki field outside Moscow, each flight monitored for everything from pilot's blood pressure to urine output. There were some secrets the Russians knew about how to fly their Sukhois that made all the difference. How to bump it around corners, for instance, or how to set it on a line. Guys like Mikhail Mamistov were almost autopilots. Mamis-

tov had already won a world championship in glider aerobatics. Now, switched over to power planes, he was ruthless with
himself. During painful outside pushes he would hold eight,
nine, ten negative g's without flinching. You knew from watching that the blood had to be bursting against the inside of his
ears and his eyes. Other pilots watching would say "ouch" as
he flew around an outside corner. But there was no hint of
backing off as you watched the plane in the sky. It was as if
someone had punched in "Ten Negative" and he was simply
along for the painful ride. The Russian camps were all about
passing on the secret knowledge that made that possible, little
mysteries of the Sukhois and of parts of the aerodynamic envelope no engineer could explain. Mind control too. The best
sports psychology work had been done by men like Alexander
Romen who had taught a generation of Russian athletes to relax on command, like Pavlov's dogs at the bell. There was
none of the charm of the French training experience here.
The Russian drill was like a KGB training school you might
read about in Le Carré, Soviet agents mastering the secret
tools of murder before disappearing into a misty Berlin midnight. The Russians flew with urgency, as if a loss might mean
a call from Moscow or a long train ride to Siberia. They hadn't
yet shaken the fear from their flying. Not of the planes, but of
the world outside that cockpit.

They weren't all ugly. In fact, possibly the most beautiful
woman ever to fly aerobatics was a member of the 2001
Russian team. Svetlana Kapanina was a former gymnast. Just
over thirty years old, she had been one of the dominant
women pilots in the world for a half decade. Hennaed hair, a

beguiling smile, a wicked outside snap roll. World competitions were still segregated. All the pilots flew together but a separate men's and women's championship was awarded. This rattled some of the women, of course. Debby Rihn-Harvey, an icon of American aerobatics who had flown on eight U.S. national teams, found it slightly annoying. And it was a little ridiculous when you thought of pilots like Patty Wagstaff, who had won the U.S. championship outright three times. But there was really nothing to be done. Not until the women started beating the men at Worlds. Then maybe an adjustment would occur. Kapanina, her last name was all most people used, was giving it a run. She routinely finished in the top ten overall, beating out dozens of hapless men. In 1998, she nearly won the whole contest. And she looked as if she belonged on the French team, a head-turning beauty not averse to peeling away her flight suit to show a T-shirt for the photographers. The Lithuanian team, largely beefy men with dumb looks on their faces, stopped all conversation when she walked by. Spanish pilots checked the mirror discreetly tucked into their training tent. The French winked.

So there was David Martin from the Possum Kingdom in Texas soaring straight up through the Spanish sky. It was day four of the 2001 World Championships. The heat in Burgos was unreal. But everyone was watching, standing outside their tents in the white sun. He was flying the last flight of this round, a privilege given to the man who finished the prior flight in first place. David Martin had won the first two flights. That left him with two flights more before the World Championship would be his. Sixty of his competitors watched from the ground. Quietly. There were moments of brilliance in Martin's flight. *Just like Leo.* Beautiful Eddy Dussau was jammed down in third place. He had flown well in the early going, but not quite well enough to beat Martin. He stood by his red plane, neck cracked back, foie gras ogling possum.

The unknown had some complex figures, but nothing Martin hadn't seen before. The French had submitted an outside loop with an eight-point roll at the bottom. That meant pushing about six negative g's from level flight, working around a loop and plugging through a roll with eight little stops halfway through. The figure, which David and the Americans knew the French had been madly practicing, was difficult on a couple of counts. First nailing eight points in a plane that rolls at 420 degrees a second was hard. Doing it while pushing outside, your body groaning up against the straps, was a riddle. Even a tiny bit of extra rudder during the roll would snap the plane offline, into an angry zero. A similar figure had nuked Robert Armstrong's chances at the 1998 World Contest.

The United States figure had also been accepted into the unknown program. It was a devious little fucker, worthy of the French. An outside three-quarter loop that started from upside down, spun through an outside snap roll, and ended with the plane headed straight up. Once on that line the pilot had to perform an outside three-quarter snap roll. There was a murmur in the jury room when the U.S. presented the figure, then an argument. Was it too much to ask of a pilot? The fast rotation of the snap combined with the negative g forces and the whip-sharp stop would shake the pilot around like a soda. The Americans knew it was like the figure they were planning to suggest. Sometimes it baffled even them. It was eventually accepted by the jury and placed fifth in the sequence. And it wasn't like you could just fly it and land. Six more figures followed.

Martin sailed through the first two figures. Hit a level line inverted and pushed out. The judges would give him a pretty open chance. They knew him, knew his plane, were willing to consider him as a possible champion. It wasn't that they marked down the new guys, exactly, but somehow new guys never won. *You'd have to fly 15 percent better than me to win*, the veterans told rookies. And it was true. This was David's fourth appearance before the world judges. He was seasoned enough to win. So was Dussau, though. To say nothing of Kirby or Robert Armstrong or another half-dozen pilots. Though there were more than fifty flyers at the World Championships, only about fifteen were serious competitors.

Martin pushed through his three-quarter outside loop. From the ground you could hear the engine whining as it fought against the negative g's. As always in watching aerobatics there was a short delay while the sound reached the ground. It could be disconcerting at times. Martin would pull the power back to idle, go into a tail slide, and the sound of the dying engine wouldn't reach the ground before he'd finished the next figure in sequence. Martin hit the downline and settled in for the snap roll. He paused for a moment, let the plane stick on the line, and jammed in full left rudder. Oh, shit. Wrong way. Zero. The groans from the American tent had ended before the sound of his mistake came radiating down to the ground. Go home.

If it was any consolation, and it wasn't, Dussau zeroed almost the same figure the next day, on the final flight, flying in first place. A crushing mental error. It was enough to kick him from first place down to third. Mamistov, the Russian machine, cranked through to gold. David Martin finished in seventh; Kirby ninth. And in second place, to everyone's astonishment but his own, was Robert Bruce Armstrong of Athens, Georgia. Flying his ten-year-old CAP 231, a plane so old the French were frankly embarrassed to see it at the competition, he had managed a perfect sequence to lock in silver. It was the best finish by an American pilot since 1988. Armstrong enjoyed it enough that he even stopped complaining about the cost of his hotel room for a couple of hours. Sitting in his cockpit, he pointed gleefully at his g-meter, which showed plus and minus ten g's. "I kind of went to sleep there for a while," he joked about one of the hard inside pulls that had almost blacked him out. He was able to keep flying by instinct, living out the mantra that great pilots don't need to see to fly. They can hear it in their heads, the whispery saxophone music of how they want to fly. They see a beauty that at once has nothing and everything to do with their planes.

When I was twelve,
my parents sent me off
to camp in Arizona.

When I was twelve, my parents sent me off to camp in Arizona. One night for a celebration the counselors took a dozen or so of us out to a minigolf joint jammed against the highway that ran toward Phoenix. It was one of those iconic desert nights: calm, cool like an ocean. The sky looked impenetrable from under the umbrella of the minigolf lights. You knew there were stars out there. The lights obscured them. Under the minigolf lights everything was a little orange. We ran around on the fake grass and sipped Coca-Colas. On one hole I hit my ball and then stood off to the side, looking idly out at the freeway, the cars streaking by. Adults. Another world there. A motorcycle slowed down as it passed. A van smashed the cyclist from behind, throwing him through the air. Behind me, someone hit a ball into a hole.

So this is how death comes, I learned. A peaceful perfect night. You slow down for a moment and suddenly you are gone. The flash froze me for a few minutes. I watched as the ambulance came. People quit playing golf and clustered around the little wooden fence that ran along the highway. It was chipped and eroded by the heat and desert wind. Some-day, someone would have to come out and sand it down, prime it, and repaint it. It was covered with big splinters, the size of straws. Someone else had seen the accident too. A girl counselor. She seemed impossibly old, but was probably nine-teen. In the van on our way back we collapsed sobbing into each other.

I am about to describe a man's death. I cannot find a deli-cate way to say these things. You slow down for a moment and the car comes up from behind and you don't hear anything, do you? Or does time dilate in that moment, so that to die instantly is no different than to die slowly, after a long illness. Does the speed matter? I had a teacher who died of throat cancer. When the doctors had finally given him up he had a few months to collect himself. He wrote a letter to some friends and students. "See you later?" it ended. It would be nice to have that kind of time to examine your death. Or would it be terrifying?

I can see forever. It is early afternoon, Oklahoma below me. New Mexico lingers ahead. The sky is mostly clear except for dark mushrooms of rain miles off. With gentle turns, I steer between them. As I near the Four Hills pass that leads through the Rockies and into the river basin around Albu-querque, the rain showers chase me. I cut their corners and they spatter my canopy. New Mexico summer days begin clear, but the hot sun bakes the southern part of the state, pulling water into giant thunderheads that unload in late afternoon. At night, the rainwater drains south. In the morn-ing, the cycle starts again. On a hot day the convection of the desert floor can push the cumulonimbus clouds up into the sky at more than 10,000 feet an hour. Thunderheads encircle Albuquerque like guard posts as I arrive.

I put the plane up on a wing and slip around a cloud bank that hovers over the edge of the city. The air traffic controllers route me west of town before turning me in behind a Southwest 737 and a flight of F-16s returning from a training run. I have time to idly orbit over Double Eagle airport, a small field by Rio Rancho, named after the big silver balloon that carried two New Mexico pilots across the Atlantic in 1978. Maxie Anderson, one of the pilots, had inscribed a book to me when I was twelve: "Dreams always take wing." Ben Abruzzo, the other pilot, had been a family friend. Both dead now flying. Fast deaths. Anderson, ballooning, was hit by a thermal that collapsed his canopy. The cockpit fell 15,000 feet. Abruzzo died when an engine cut out on his twin, loaded with his wife, two friends, and a weekend's baggage. A lifetime's dreams.

But what beautiful ambition the two of them had, to fly a balloon across the ocean. How could you even come up with an idea like that in land-locked New Mexico? Something in the sky there breeds dreams. Cortez saw wonderful cities of gold in the reflection of the sun; Oppenheimer, terrifying cities of glass. The sadness of the state is that the dreams are so rarely made real. Something about the place makes the failure that is part of every success intolerable. Perhaps it is the beauty. A place where God's perfection is so manifest makes man's fallibility harder to accept. Every night the wonder is written in the sunsets.

Approach clears me in. I settle down behind a tight spread

of F-16s, the "lawn dart" jets of the New Mexico Air National
Guard. They go by an easy-to-remember call sign: "Taco One
and Taco Two, you're clear runway eight."

No one who loves me likes my flying aerobatics. My parents least of all. They meet me nervously at the airport. The
plane is beautiful, they say. It is a scary-looking thing, but the
lines are so elegant that they surpass the danger. The plane is
like a dagger I once saw in a museum in Florence, pure art.
My grandfather comes out to see the plane too. In World War
II he volunteered to join the Army Air Corps. He needn't have
gone. With a wife and child he was low on the draft list. He
enlisted shortly after the war began and went to flight school
in Texas. The initial training went well. He accumulated the
hours to move up to more advanced planes. On his final
check-ride, however, the instructor didn't like something
about his spin. He went up and tried it again. The Air Corps
was heavy on pilots at that point in the war, so trainees could
get bounced for the smallest of errors. My grandfather was
bounced for his spins. It probably didn't help that he had
crashed a plane on landing early in his training, overeagerly
correcting a crosswind. So off to navigator school. Then to
the front. He was twenty-six when he first flew above occupied Europe. "Thick," he would say of the antiaircraft fire he
faced there. "Like you could walk on it. And black. And sudden." Planes around him would explode in a heartbeat.
Friends dead at flamespeed. Once, on landing, he was told to
report to the commander. He was given a complex navigation
test and passed with such high marks that he was transferred
into a lead plane, one of the pathfinder B-24s that spear-

headed most missions. Two sorties later his old plane was shot down. Every one of his crewmates was killed. He came home untouched after two years.

"You don't see many wives at these things," Alan Bush had said to me once about contests. There were a few exceptions, like David Martin's wife, Martha, or Kirby's wife, Kellie. In the male-dominated sport, pilots arrived and competed alone. Partly this was because the sport bored non-pilots. Watching the same sequences over and over, performed with differences only barely discernible from the ground. But in many cases the men had simply made a decision to tuck the activity behind a mask, into a quiet corner of their lives. "If my wife really understood this," one fellow pilot coughed at me over beers one night, "the plane would be for sale tomorrow."

I thought Julie could help explain it to my family. She was an Albuquerque doctor, familiar to my father. She had been on the U.S. aerobatic team for a half decade in the 1980s, before giving up the sport. She was close to the icons of aerobatics. She was calm and wonderful. One windy afternoon I took my dad over to visit Julie and her husband, Scoop, in their hangar. The couple were deep into the required one-hundred-hour inspections of the two T-6 trainers they flew together in airshows. The planes were stripped down and squared bolts from the big radial engines were neatly arranged on the giant gray wings. Julie and Scoop passed tools back and forth. Joked about whose plane would be finished first. Julie had abandoned her medical practice to spend more time flying with Scoop, who was a former airline pilot. As rain began beating down on the metal hangar roof, a drumroll that slowly drowned out our conversation, Julie explained to my father what made the sport safe. She told him how, by paying such careful attention to our planes, we tried to remove as much of the risk as possible. How we practiced high even if we performed low. Alan Bush had flown with her on the U.S. team. *I couldn't have found a better coach.* It was all simply a matter of care. Of never letting the plane get away from you. Of never forgetting the plane would kill you for incaution or arrogance.

I had seen Julie and Scoop flying together one morning over the mesa where I practiced. As I left the FAA-designated aerobatic box, they came in. They were flying the most difficult kind of aerobatics, in formation with each other. There were limits on what the heavy T-6s could do with their WWII-era wings, but within those limits, the flying was beautiful. Together they would soar up, wingspans apart, before pivoting earthward again. Below us, along the still-chill Rio Grande basin, a few hot air balloons lifted off for short morning flights. I twisted my plane upside down to watch the balloons for a moment, then right side up to stare at Julie and Scoop again.

The rain picked up its pace, hitting the hangar roof like load after load of buckshot. Suddenly there was no sound left for conversation. Julie and Scoop wished us well. *Stay calm at Nationals. Don't think too much.* We stared at the black sky together, looking through an opening in the hangar door.

Then Julie took up her tools again. I ran out in the rain and pulled up the car. My dad and I drove off. "She seems more beautiful and happy than I've ever seen her," he said quietly. I agreed. And somehow this sentiment rubbed off on my flying. My father, who had opposed my even getting a license when I was in school, told me how the very impenetrability of my desires made my efforts inspiring, not terrifying. We drove home as the thunderstorm beat out its fury against our car windows.

Three days later I was up early. It was an ideal morning, just cool enough to manage a good flight. Afterward, a breakfast burrito at the Frontier on Central Avenue, the old Route 66. I grabbed the morning paper as I walked out. AIRSHOW PILOT KILLED IN RATON. Scoop, said the lower left-hand corner, was dead. With Julie watching from her plane, he had nosed into the ground out in the thin-aired northern town where they were preparing for an airshow. He had just started a low-level steep wingover, a high-performance turn that sent the plane knifing nearly straight up. As he pulled up hard onto a vertical line the engine had coughed hard, leaving him without power. "My engine just quit," he radioed. It came at a terrible moment, with the plane loaded up with g's, its tail pointing down. The figure, which can be finished with almost no altitude to spare, is one of the sexiest an airshow pilot can fly. But if there is a problem, it's one of the most lethal. A dead engine might be the worst problem you could have in this situation.

In other circumstances, if you were in the traffic pattern, say, you might just be able to glide in after an engine failure. Scoop had been almost right above the airport when his engine stopped. But as he furiously pushed the plane around to try to get it flying again, the engine caught on and sputtered back with full power. The sudden torque twisted the old plane around hard on its back and, before he had time to recover, into the ground. It was five-thirty in the afternoon. There was nothing to be done. Also dead was the twenty-six-year-old along for a ride.

My good, sensitive father was reduced to tears, thinking of Julie's lost happiness. My mother's stoicism was betrayed by red eyes, a quiver in her back, tightness in her words. We tried simply to acknowledge this awful moment and move on. Not possible. I went out and flew anyway. Fuck you.

The next morning I left for training camp. I loaded up my plane with gas and headed toward Oklahoma through quiet morning skies. There was no chatter on the radios, little traffic. I thought about Julie, still up at Raton, and I wondered how she would get her plane back to Albuquerque. I flew past a place in the Sandias where a flight instructor of mine had died years before, disoriented in a cloudbank. I flew over La Cueva canyon, a little east-west crevice in the face of the mountains named for the little cave halfway up. La Cueva was where I taught myself to rock-climb, often without a rope. It was where I hiked every time I came home, long exhausting walks that took me up past where the trail ended and sent me home with legs scratched bloody and my face caked with salty sweat and dirt. La Cueva, where I had made love to girls near the small waterfall that had been working against the rock there for millennia, making it so smooth you could hardly get a grip to get past the water. La Cueva, where I want my ashes scattered when my time comes.

I suppose the one thing my parents could never understand was that if anything did happen to me, it would be all right with me. I have had more happiness in some hours of my life than many people have in their entire allotted time. If it all ended now, I thought, I would be okay. "It's worth it in the end," the French pilot Mermoz told his friend Saint Exupéry. "The final smashup. It's worth it." I had been blessed with a chance to live and love and fly, which was really an expression of all those things. An end was inevitable, one way or another. Better fast than slow.

Sunday afternoon, late.

Sunday afternoon, late. I touch down gently at Clarence Page Airport, tucked into the southwest corner of Oklahoma City, hard along the Interstate. I've flown most of the way along Interstate 40 from Albuquerque, the route I once traced from home to college in Chicago every fall. There was a time when I could name every good truck-driver's strip club between Amarillo and St. Louis. I have fond memories of Oklahoma, a land of dancing coeds and cheap Budweiser. Once I was three days late for school.

From the traffic pattern overhead I can see an aerobatic box, staked out with big white plastic markers in the airport infield. The field itself is dead silent when I arrive. I taxi past the airport office, looking for a sign of the other pilots who are supposed to be meeting me here for a training camp. Nothing. I kill the engine, unstrap my chute, and wander around the ghostly parking strip. A light sprinkle begins to show on my Plexiglas canopy, showers that I had raced across the Texas panhandle catching up with me. From a distant hangar come a few pained strains of Willie Nelson. With the rain starting, I worry about putting the plane up for the night. Extras store rainwater in places where it has to be drained by hand. I look around again. Nothing in sight. I sigh, put my parachute back on, and prepare to fly fifteen minutes north to

Wiley Post Airport, where I hope I can find an indoor hangar.
I am whistling Willie Nelson.

"Clear." I crank the engine and tighten my straps before I
taxi out to the runway. I hear a loud buzz overhead as a Sukhoi
31, blue and yellow, shoots through to the landing pattern.
"Hey, down there," comes a voice on the radio. "Where you
goin'?" Ah, now, this is familiar. I stab my left rudder, wheel
the plane around, and taxi back to the ramp.

The Sukhoi belongs to Keith, a thirty-something busi-
nessman from California. It is a lovely brute of a plane, the
newest Sukhoi model and one of the last planes to come off
the assembly lines before Soviet-style bankruptcy hit Sukhoi.
I follow Keith off the taxiway as a white rental car screams up.
Jim, a Las Vegas dentist and Extra pilot, meets up with us and
we pull in behind him as he drives south on the field. Last year
Jim had to bail out of his plane after a control failure. It ended
up in a heap on the desert floor; he was quickly back flying.
Keith and Jim have been winning trophies at West Coast
competitions for most of the spring. Both are hopeful for
Nationals. They have been training with Sergei Boriak for a
couple of years and hew to an exhausting a routine. Up early,
four flights, dinner, bed. Jim's car is packed with the parapher-
nalia of hard training: chocolate Power Bars and berry-
flavored Gatorade, extra engine oil and spare bolts. I'll be
here three days with them and Hubie Tolson, an Unlimited
pilot from North Carolina, before moving deeper into Oklahoma to meet up with Alan Bush at yet another camp, this one
closer still to the Nationals site at Dennison.

In an annual ritual, pilots from around the United States

are clustering on small fields in Oklahoma and Texas for last-minute training camps with coaches like Sergei. Pilots who don't have the time or money to book a coach train with each other, radioing suggestions back and forth. There is an ethos in the sport that everyone helps everyone else. You want to win by flying your best flight against another pilot's best flight, so the advice is almost always honest. We all make three or four flights a day in the heat, which regularly passes 100 degrees. On any given day in September, in a fifty-mile radius of Dennison there are several dozen pilots jamming performance from their planes, looking feverishly for holes in their flying, the dark spots in their planes' envelopes. It is better to find them here, in front of friends, than later in front of judges. Better to find them at 3,000 feet than 300. It is punishing work, and by the end of the day most of us are walking around stiff and exhausted, a little dazed. There are moments of wonder, though, like the occasional sensation of holding on to our planes as they fly.

How to train? Theories abound. Fifteen minutes of figure after figure according to a plan you've worked out on the ground? Repeat your known sequence over and over? Fly figures as they are barked out to you from the ground, preparation for the unknowns? These flights are repetitive: five rolls, five snaps, five spins, and so on. First, man is an ass, Nietzsche wrote of learning, struggling with the burden of what he must know. Then, a lion, master of what he has learned. Finally, man becomes a child, free of all assumptions, free to create anew. So with our flying. We seek the instinctive, the creative. Thousands of pilots have managed the mechanical skills of moving the plane around certain figures, one after another. Great pilots do something else, though. They can visualize their flights, which allows them to use their imagination to create. You can sense it from their first figure. Is this going to be exciting or not? Their shapes mark their minds no less clearly than lines from a love letter mark our hearts.

Keith and I taxi up to an old WWII hangar and kill our engines. Silence lowers onto the field as the rain continues lightly. Our conversations echo into the old hangars and out again.

"Good flight in?"

"I was right behind you in Amarillo, did you see me?"

"The controllers were asking me if we were going to the same place."

Jim cranks a hangar open and we carefully roll our planes in for the night. Sergei pulls up in a rented minicar, straight from Dennison where he has been coaching other pilots. We head toward Oklahoma City for dinner, sleep, and a six A.M. reunion at the Cracker Barrel restaurant near our hotels. Sergei will be there early.

Deep breath. The sweat is beating down into my eyes. Some has dripped onto my sunglasses. The drops are a kaleidoscope that refracts the sky and earth as they blur past. Deep breath. Sergei is on the radio. He is unhappy with my rolls. "Look, show me roll entry again." I pull the plane around in a tight left circle and level off hard at 1,500 feet. It is roasting hot.

Both cockpit vents are open, squirting high-altitude air at my face. I pull back fast on the stick, putting the plane on a 45-degree lineup. "Okay," Sergei says, his voice crackling a bit through static. "Full deflection." I roll the plane fast and stop inverted. I climb, upside down now, for a few seconds and then tuck the plane at the ground. I extend the line down, taking a fast look out over the left wing to ensure I am lined up vertically. One thousand feet. I pull level. A jagged line in the sky, a half triangle called a Shark's Tooth.

"Was that full deflection?" Sergei asks. Did I put the stick over to the side of the cockpit as fast and hard as possible, he is asking. Did I throw it over?

"More or less," I say.

"Nooo," he whines in his accented English, Pushkin lamenting a lost draft. "I don't want to hear 'more or less.' You're supposed to be fool, fool deflection. All the way to the stop. Stick all the way to the stop. Take your two hands, take hand off throttle and put both hands on stick. Put it all the way to the side. You're supposed to feel the stop, where stick hits end of range."

I level again. Pop the 45 degrees up and roll. Harder this time. The plane is rolling so fast now that it feels out of control. "Good, better," Sergei says in my ear. "Go again. Maximum rate of roll. Go as low as you are comfortable." In Sergei-speak "maximum" comes out as "max-ee-mum." I set for another pull, blink stinging sweat from my eyes. Again the world flies around me, I go around in just over a second. "Pull. Good. No, stick to the stop! Can you imagine, stick to the stop! Don't slow down. It can rotate much faster but you have to use stick to the stop. You are wasting energy. Only one choice: maximum deflection and as aggressive as possible. Pull up forty-five degrees and fast roll." I hit it. "Okay, not too bad. Can be even faster."

"Fuck," I mutter to myself. I am rolling the plane as fast as I can and still keep it in control. My last time around the wings coughed a bit as I started past horizontal, symptoms of a tip-stall in which the wingtips are moving so fast they quit flying altogether. It is hard to force myself to move the stick faster. The plane can take it, of course, but the speed becomes quickly disorienting, making the roll harder to stop. Something is wrong with my technique too and I am spilling out of the rolls inelegantly. I am trying to throw a curve ball without knowing how my fingers should wrap the seams. I roll my head around in the cockpit, loosening my neck. I flip upside down for a moment and then put the plane up on the right wing with a fast roll and pull around in a six-g turn, flying back toward Sergei at 1,000 feet. He is sitting below me, right along the runway, staring up through his Revos. As I come in, he begins talking again. He likes the rolls performed right at him since it allows him to see all the mistakes more clearly. He is good enough, though, to pick up errors from any angle. He likes to joke about flying the plane by remote control, telling me what to do to correct my errors. He is so familiar with aerobatic flight that he can see an unnecessary pound of foot-pressure on the rudder, an extra finger on the stick.

"Okay, look, if you spend money and pay hundred and whatever thousand bucks and you use the plane for only twenty-five thousand dollars, what is that?" He pauses and then answers his own question. "Stewpeed." I can hear him swallowing Gatorade, water, something. Something cool. I am level. "Use *full* performance of plane," he says, spitting the word "full." I pull up to 45 degrees and push forward to lock my line in. "Now, stick to the side as aggressive as possible. To the maxeemum. That's correct." The sky and earth whirl around too fast but somehow I recover when I am supposed to. No tip-stall.

"Okay," Sergei says. "Faster. Faster. Ees not twenty-five-thousand-dollar plane, okay?"

The conceit of the Soviet system that produced men like Sergei, its seduction too, was: we can control everything. No surprises. How many acres of corn do we need next fall? Let's plan it out and grow that much corn. How many violinists? How many figure skaters? How many aerobatic pilots? Someone come up with a list, a system. You could evaporate chance from human life this way, the planners said. It was a wonderful system, they thought. Stultified. Straitened. It was hard to be a blazing success at anything. Blazing we don't want. Planned, okay? The whole country was about *planned* production. Was it too much to ask that its citizens' lives be planned too?

So here was how they systematized aerobatics: They rounded up the best pilots they could find, stuck them in a lab, and tried to figure out what made them excellent. Was it eye color? Height? Could they read fast? No, the tests concluded, in the end it was all about reaction time. Throw a ball at these pilots and their hands moved faster than their fellow Soviets. Clap your hands behind them and they turned around faster. So the word went out: find us kids with fast reaction times. We need this many of them.

Sergei Boriak was a kid in Kazakhstan who liked flying. By the time he was in his early teens he was skipping school to stand at the local airport and gape at the planes as they came and went on military maneuvers or ferried important officials around. The chance to wash a dirty Antonov could get him humming for a week. He would walk around the airfield like it was his own, in that strange possessive way that teen boys have. Whistling and smiling and helping with planes. He began fiddling around as a mechanic and decided that what he really wanted to do was fly. This wasn't easy. The Soviet system needed only a few pilots. Sergei fought his way through the initial training and screening, where 15 of 300 pilots were allowed through. And once he was through, once in the door, he was never leaving. When he wasn't flying he would talk about flying. He would work on planes. Anything to be near them. You might see Sergei strolling around the airport. Perhaps he would be flipping a wrench in the air. If you looked carefully you might notice something: he was catching it damn fast.

He had it. That was all you could say. The reaction thing. Boriak had it in spades. He seemed even built for it. A small, compact wrestler's body that moved like a well-oiled crane. He used the shortest amount of time and energy to do anything: shake hands, comb his hair, smile. Everything was like an on-off switch. You want to tuck your shirt in? The machine whirs into action, makes a few quick gestures, then settles down. He was a neuromuscular research geek's dream, all precision movement and intensity. He could have been a robot really. He could be taught to do anything, the coaches thought. He was a wonderboy. Years later this is how other pilots would still refer to him: wonderboy.

So the Soviet system, in its wisdom, reached deep into Kazakhstan and grabbed Sergei Boriak and changed his life. The meeting with the talent spotter. The tests. The eyes on his body, his hands, his face. Notes in the files. *Look how he moves.* The victories at the regional contests began at once. The total mastery of complexity. The best they had ever seen, judges said. And then the offer, the chance to become the youngest member of the Soviet aerobatic team.

Boriak came close to winning the World Championship once. 1988. He had won the first two flights at the Worlds. Two flights to go. In the third he was in the middle of a maneuver, flying straight up, when he heard a crackle on the radio. "Land," the voice said. He broke off his routine mid-flight, whipped around into the traffic pattern and landed. Had another plane strayed into the box? Was there something wrong on the officiating line? Why had they interrupted his flight? He was wondering what had happened as he killed the engine and rolled up to the chief judge. Who was also wondering what was going on.

"Why did you land?"

"Someone told me to, on the radio."

"Well, it wasn't us."

Boriak was zeroed. The ghost transmission. A member of an opposing team? A plane on the wrong frequency. It didn't matter. Boriak had lost his chance to be world champion.

He might have had another, if he wanted. If he would have stayed inside the Russian training organization. Kept living in Moscow. Struggled. Others did it. But by 1992 the wall between East and West was coming down. Boriak wanted to be on the other side. He had made a few contacts on the American and European team during his time as a competitor. They weren't easy to manage. Sergei didn't speak English. The KGB hovered around him. *Where are you going, Sergei?* A walk. *Yes, it would be a nice night to get some air. Perhaps I will join you.* But he would manage sometimes to get out for a drink with the Western pilots. He would chat them up, all sign language and enthusiasm, between flights. *Where are you going, Sergei?* To look at the capitalists' planes. The Americans knew Boriak was a shit-hot pilot, but they began to see something else burning in his eyes. Something other than competition. It was hope, as a kind of question.

In the late 1980s, the U.S.S.R. started selling a few aerobatic planes to the West. They needed the hard currency and aerobatic planes were one of the few things Russia had that the world wanted. The Sukhois were huge machines. Massively overpowered by 360-hp radial engines, they could get airborne in less than 700 feet. They were so solid you could do anything with them: fly inverted at ten feet above the ground, take your hands off the stick. But the Russian engineering was a cipher to American engineers. If you wanted to buy a Sukhoi, the line went, buy two. One to work on, one to fly. And also get a Russian to work on them.

Boriak could do that. He knew Sukhois the way you might

know your father's last words: memorized, each one resonant with memory. For Boriak it was the plane that had transformed him from a Kazakh farm boy into a Hero of the Soviet Union. He loved it, admired its brutality, cherished its reputation. He had been the plane's first test pilot.

At the time it wasn't clear if this was an honor or an insult. Did they simply consider him the most expendable pilot they could find? He had just been talent-spotted by the Soviet coaches a year before. The more senior members of the team were training for the world competition in their Yakovlevs, an older and slower plane. Sergei got a tap on the shoulder. Sukhoi had decided to get into the aerobatic plane business and it wanted a pilot to try and break their plane. This might be a little too easy to do. Sukhoi engineers—Russia's finest, sculptors of the country's most lethal fighters—weren't really that interested in aerobatics. What was drawing them to the little Su-26 was the idea of using composites instead of metal to build planes. What will happen if we mount a ludicrous amount of horsepower on a flyweight airplane? They didn't want to answer this question with a $200 million jet fighter. "Send us a pilot," they said to the Soviet aerobatic foundation. Sergei Boriak arrived. "I was dummy pilot," he said later. They gave him long sheets of yes/no questions to answer on each flight. Finally, when all the checklists lined up and made the engineers happy, he became the first pilot to compete in the plane. Then the huge honor of being the first pilot to fly the Sukhoi in front of a crowd in the West. It was 1987. In front of a skeptical European crowd he flew ten consecutive snap rolls straight at the ground, a maniacal feat of total fearlessness.

He met Randy Gagne at one of the world contests and immediately recognized a kindred spirit in the Canadian. They spoke about three words in common, but they didn't need more than that. Slowly, when the eyes were off him, Sergei let Randy know he might be interested in crossing over, in coming out of Russia. The Wall fell. And in 1992, Gagne brought Sergei to the United States. Randy was many things, but financially stable wasn't one of them. He was a wonderful pilot, whose huge, happy spirit seemed to survive even after he was killed in an Extra. He was generous with Boriak and introduced him around, which was how he caught the eye of Hubie Tolson, a North Carolina furniture baron who had a bought a Sukhoi that he couldn't find anyone to fix. Tolson was a character too. He had run away from home at seventeen to join the airshow business. He flew for the pure joy of the thing. Once, as a kid, he found a new, unopened road running for miles. He took his plane down to the ground, bounced his wheels on the asphalt, popped up into a roll, and then bounced again. If it hadn't been for the guy in the woods it would have been a fun trick. The guy in the woods called the FAA. Hubie was grounded for a year.

It was a blessing. It forced him to get serious about life. To settle down. But twenty years later he was ready to fly again, to compete. And the only man in the West who knew how to fly a Sukhoi the way he wanted was Boriak. Tolson paved Boriak's way into American life. Tolson helped him get a green card, bringing him in under a provision that allowed visas to foreigners who were in the "top 5 percent" in their field worldwide. Brain surgeons. Electrical engineers. Sergei. They sent photocopies of Sergei's medals to the INS, letters from American pilots, pictures of Sergei flying inverted with the ground in the background. Hubie helped Sergei set up a business, pick prices for his training, learn English. It took a while for the demand to grow. In the mid-1990s Boriak was spending more time doing lawn care in North Carolina than coaching. But by 1996 the business began to pick up. Hubie helped Boriak bring his family over. Then helped him move to Washington, D.C., where Sergei swapped dental work for flight training with a local dentist, who later killed himself performing a benefit airshow in front of a crowd of schoolchildren.

What Boriak brought to American aerobatics was serious coaching. He hadn't been trained just to fly. The Soviet system had also taught him to teach, sent him back to Kazakhstan with the mission of building more Sergei Boriaks. Americans were used to coaches who had never flown Unlimited, men who often berated the pilots out of frustration with what they couldn't do themselves. Sergei changed all that. By 1996 he was the official coach for the American team. He was on the road more than 150 days a year. His English got better. And flying with him was about as much of a guarantee as you could get. If you did what he said, you would get better. If you did what he said, you would start to win.

"Look, fly faster." Keith looks at me. He stares for a moment at his feet, stuck into black neoprene racing shoes—fireproof and common on Sukhoi pilots. "Brother, you can't hurt the plane. And you're killing yourself flying slow up there." Every flight I push the plane harder, but I am so new that I often end up behind the plane. Flying at 150 knots, I feel as if I could keep up at 140. By the time I feel happy at 150, Sergei is shouting for 170. Keith presses me for 200. "Get on the plane. Get on it hard. You can't hurt the plane."

When I come screaming into the box to start my flight, barreling down from 4,000 feet to 2,300, I have two things: altitude and energy. From the moment I enter the box I will be trading one off against the other. My first figure is a hard pull up to vertical that will shoot me a couple of thousand feet up. But when I push the plane over the top, I will have almost no energy. To regain it, I'll spin into a vertical dive. For the whole sequence I'll be swapping back and forth: altitude, energy, altitude, energy. An aerobatic plane is like a pebble tossed into the air, the Swiss champion Erich Müller used to explain. When it slows at the very top of its flight, it has traded all of its airspeed for altitude. When it smacks back down toward earth, it has swapped the altitude for speed. I am like a rug merchant in the air, holding a canny negotiation, trading speed against altitude, managing both.

By flying any slower than flat out, I'm robbing myself. The tiny stylistic mistakes in figure after figure are a felony. Collectively they may cost me a dozen miles an hour during a five-minute flight. Trivial anywhere but in an aerobatics box. Sergei wants a fast roll from me because anything less than full deflection is a waste of energy. The faster I fly, the more energy I conserve, the better my exchange rate between altitude and airspeed.

The slow figures are particularly killing me on my spin. As I fumble along trying to slow the plane down to spin, I am kicking it left and right, pissing away extra energy by bouncing my rudder into the slipstream and out again. The plane is skewing to the side, instead of dropping straight down. Not much of a wobble, maybe 5 degrees. Unnoticeable to anyone but an expert. Since I am only flying a one-rotation spin, the Extra doesn't have enough time to get into a clean, fully developed spin. That means every aerodynamic mistake is magnified by the time I can correct it. Instead of a clean entry, the plane stutters through a dirty stall, into a turbulent back flip, followed by a spiral and, when I recover, a nosedive. I should be entering the spin straight ahead, like going through a door. For some reason I'm nursing the plane to the right, something Sergei can see.

He watches each flight from under the shade of an umbrella. Jim, Keith, and I fly one right after another for about twenty minutes each. Sergei talks to us on the radio and also into a tape recorder. When we land we sit in his air-conditioned rental car and review the tapes, visualizing our flights again and listening to Sergei's advice. On the first morning he stops my sequence after one spin and has me spin for twenty minutes, until I am nearly out of gas. He begins by telling me to climb up and then dictates control movements to me over the radio. "Rudder in now!" he says. "Forward elevator." It is not working. I am not feeling the lurch that comes with a good spin, the sensation of the plane falling away, no longer flying. I am not following him closely enough. Sergei has me climb to 4,000 feet and put the plane in an extended spin. I hit the rudder and begin turning. One, two, three, four rotations. The plane spins faster as it wraps up, as the wings finally quit flying. At 2,000 feet he calls out the recovery inputs. I climb up and do it again. Five rotations. Six. Then back to the one-rotation competition spin. I slam it hard, paste the downline exactly on heading. A revelation.

I land and walk over to the car, past a collection of students from the local high school who have come out to watch us fly. "I feel like I'm kicking my way through the first three-quarters of the spin," I complain. "It's like I jam in the rudder, but that's the only thing keeping it going around. The wing doesn't feel stalled."

"Yes, yes," Sergei says. "You have to remember on a one-rotation spin that you have to have clean entry into the stall. Otherwise you are not really spinning. If you stall plane clean, you will have perfect condition for recovery." He is smiling in his reassuring way. "Perfect condition," he repeats.

"Okay, but I'm finding I'm having to climb a little bit to get a clean entry," I say. It's not much, but the nose rises as I enter the stall and I worry that the judges will mark me down. By lifting the nose to keep the appearance of a straight line, I'm dragging the plane right and fouling my spin entry.

"Will I get downgraded for that?"

"No, it's absolutely normal for the nose to come up. You are thinking too much."

I wander off and find myself thinking of Lisa. A past master of aerial charm, a master of the kind of aerobatics that comes from unconscious flight, the kind of aerobatics Sergei wants from me. We would meet in the California mornings, strap into a plane together, and go to twist above the ocean until we were sipping the last of our gas. It was an addiction of sorts. She was twenty-six, I was twenty-two. Those cool Long Beach skies, waiting for us cloudless. Every figure she flew was, to me, like a sentence in another language. That was a loop? Oh yes, her flying seemed to say, that was a loop as I see it. An older woman instructing a young lover. She was beautiful, but the flying made her more so. With aerobatic figures, she was a cougar. "To the door, to the floor!" she would shout, exhorting me to roll faster and harder. It was an unusual aerobatic plane, one that allowed us to sit side by side, pressed into our seats by compression straps and gravity. Upside down, her blond hair would stream overhead as we rolled around. Always her voice would be giggling in my ears, loose and happy in the air. This was what imagination looked like in the sky, an ability to slip past simple aerodynamics into something more natural. It was the kind of thing you could spend a lifetime trying to capture again, and what Sergei was trying to teach me. It couldn't be learned, though. At least not just in the air, because it was a way of living as much as a way of flying. If you are going to put in your controls, put them all the way in. Put them to the floor, put them to the door. Roll faster, as Sergei would say. As true in life as in the air.

Equally true on a hot afternoon, when Lisa was working as a fire pilot, driving a water-bomber for the Forest Service. Dream Job. On her first day of work, as she was tugging a water-heavy plane into the air at the end of a takeoff roll, the spotter plane flying just behind her clipped off the tail of her plane. The heavy plane began a ponderous, uncontrollable roll onto its back and, seconds later, into the ground. The weight of the plane, the speed, conspired against even full controls. Live your life to the door, to the floor. Eventually the inputs are not enough. The controls feel mushy and weak and we know this is the end. But that blond hair. The giggles.

Three days with Sergei. A new set of virtues: sharp corners, smooth rolls, clean lines. Mostly he endows me with speed. No more slow, graceful ballet in the sky. The world begins to move faster. And, a surprise, the plane becomes easier to control at high speed. She wants to fly fast. This was what Walter Extra had in mind in the first place. It was what I had in mind. A bumper sticker of macho happiness: No more ballet.

"I won't get downgraded?" I wonder about some of the small fidgets I am now making to stay in the right place.

"Nooo. No, no, no. But look, you have to go into everything faster. The person who taught you spins, he doesn't care about precision. He cares that you don't crash the plane. But when you are flying the sequence you have to take care of energy management. You have to get in clean." I suck on my Gatorade for a moment. "Full inputs," Sergei says. "Can you imagine?"

You might see the knife strapped to his parachute and think to yourself, "This is ridiculous."

You might see the knife strapped to the parachute and think to yourself, "This is ridiculous." And it looks a little ludicrous, to be honest. The knife is an old Bowie, worn down and a bit rusted around the handle, where the metal is serrated like a grater to give a better grip. It is strapped onto the shoulder of Phil Knight's parachute in the way you might see a sidearm lashed to a fighter pilot's combat rig. The knife says: I AM READY FOR ACTION! It is ready to cut through tangled parachute shroud lines, to hack through a jammed canopy when the airplane is flaming earthward. It is ready! What makes it a little strange is that Phil looks like he's ready too. For some doughnuts. He is a bit lumpy in the middle, his shoulders slouch, his hair is mostly gone. He looks as soft as that knife is hard. The looks deceive.

It is July 1996. Phil is up in the sky, cranking out practice maneuvers in his Extra. He is in the running this year for the world contest. After a decade of preparation he feels this could be his year to win it all. He settles the plane down and tries an inverted outside snap, about the maximum for outside g forces, somewhere around eight negative g's. When Phil pushes forward on the stick to start the snap, his crotch strap cleaves in half from the sudden pressure, nearly 2,000 pounds delivered in less than a second. His seat then wrenches loose from the cockpit floor and Phil shoots up and through the Plexiglas canopy, using his balding head as a glass breaker. When he wakes up, he is jammed about chest-high out of the dome, his arms pinned to his sides and propeller-blasted wind in his face. He can't move up or down. His parachute is cranked down onto his back, still strapped tightly in place, holding him inside the cockpit like an expansion bolt. The plane, in the absence of any control inputs, begins heading toward the ground at full power. Phil is 1,000 feet in the air. He can't reach the stick. He tries for the throttle. He stretches his arm out as far as he can and just manages to touch it. He grabs what he can of the walnut-sized knob and pulls hard. The power reduction sucks him down into his seat. He tears the plane out of the power dive. Four hundred feet.

Bailout. That's his first thought. *Just get out.* But 400 feet won't give him nearly enough time to get out of the plane and get his chute open. And who knows what his little excursion through the glass just did to the chute. It could be stuffed with tiny bits of Plexiglas, as perforated and useless as an old rag. He is going to have to land the plane. He tries the controls, making a gentle roll one way, then the other. The plane responds smoothly. He circles back over the airport and, very gingerly, lands the plane. And straps a knife to his chest. He was never going to be pinned anywhere again. A couple of years later, Charlie Hillard, another champion pilot, dies in Lakeland, Florida, when his Sea Fury flips over after a botched landing. Charlie was trapped inside the glass bubble of his cockpit and suffocated before he could be cut loose. *If only he'd had a knife.*

But Phil is so goddamned serious, even after something like that, you might be tempted to joke about the knife, about Phil's other quirks, like his no-bullshit way of talking, his life-and-death approach to teaching aerobatics. He's not like other coaches. You might be tempted to joke: "Where does Phil think he is, 'Nam?" Conjure the image of Phil fighting off a couple of angry Florida farmers with his little knife if he ever did bail out. "I'm not going alive," he might shout in your little fantasy. Hah-hah.

Okay, asshole, as Phil might say, let me tell you about the four times I *was* shot down in Vietnam. Except he would never say that. He would never tell the stories to impress you. But let me tell you about just one trip, the night north of Saigon on the candlelight patrol. It explains Phil's intensity, explains why he stuffs his coaching with the kind of advice you'll need only if you are flying right on the very edge. The work of every artist is shaped by his life.

Nineteen sixty-five. Fall. There are three American choppers working the Vietnamese jungle on a night patrol. One is flying low, treetop level, blacked out. Another, a sitting duck, at 1,000 feet, lit up at the perfect range for the enemy guns. A third chopper is at 2,500 feet, also blacked out, armed with the heavy 50-calibers, the ones that make toothpicks from trees. You get the picture: Fool the Vietcong or the NVA or whoever the unlucky SOB is that night into thinking the spotlight chopper in the middle is out alone, hunting or lost. When Charlie opens up on the light, it gets switched off; the two other choppers open like your worst nightmare. So here's Lt. Phil Knight, fire-team leader, twenty-four-years-old, flying deep into bad-guy territory. It is a hot night. You can smell the jungle. He's the low chopper in the sandwich, flying maybe fifty feet above the trees in the dim moonlight. The black-green canopy flows underneath like a moving carpet. Then an explosion. His controls are shot away. They hadn't fooled anyone, at least not Charlie. The helicopter slams forward as if it has tripped on something, somersaulting angrily down onto the trees.

They had made two mistakes, Phil thought as he sat in the jungle waiting silently for the rescue bird. First: they had come back to the same place they had been the night before. It was tempting to do that, thinking they'd be thinking *They'll never come back a second time*. Wrong. Second: it was too bright a night. Charlie probably wasn't fooled by the searchlight trick anyhow, but it didn't make any sense to come zipping through with a moonlit background, the choppers all done up in soft white light like someone's wedding photo. Phil and his crew scrambled clear of their bird. The Huey was fully loaded: 38 rockets on the outside, 400 rounds of ammo in the guns. They had been hit before they had time to fire off a thing. Now the chopper was sitting there, cooking in a fire. They were waiting for it all to blow up, the way you might wait for a sneeze. And waiting to see if the Vietcong were coming for them.

This was how you learned in Vietnam. Mistake. Lesson. Phil and his team were among the first airborne gunship squads the Army deployed. They were an experiment, so they had to teach themselves almost everything. And the lessons were expensive. Knight shipped out with twenty-four other pilots; thirteen were dead by the time the tour was over. DON'T FLY BETWEEN 50 AND 2,500 FEET. That kind of thing would be typed up on a sheet for future generations of Vietnam-bound chopper pilots, and God knew they would be coming. Too bad it had cost some good ol' American boy his life before they figured it out. IF YOU'RE GOING TO FLY LOW, THEN FLY REALLY LOW, RIGHT ON THE TREES. That was the lesson of the moonlight disaster. Lucky it didn't cost Phil. The lessons made you a hell of a pilot if they didn't kill you in the process.

This was the true nature of gunship work, a violent dialectic in which death was your teacher. This is true of all war, of course, but for the gunship men it was an immediate lesson, a fast exchange, as quick and simple as changing dollars at the base PX. You swapped death for knowledge. If you were lucky, you could buy that same knowledge with danger instead. Either way, you went out every night looking for something to shoot at. Generally, it wanted to shoot back. It didn't help that Phil's unit was mostly doing special ops support. They'd load up outside Saigon, head off to the hills for a couple of days and live with the special forces guys in some corner of hell, flying ten hours of combat support a day. Phil flew 1,000 hours of *combat* time on his first hitch. Talking about it forty years later he still punctuates every other sentence with a sigh. Which is not like Phil Knight. Phil is aggressive. A bull of a man, born with strong opinions and the will to enforce them on the world. It's what makes him such an unforgiving aerobatics coach. But he'll admit when he's rattled. Down in the Vietnamese jungle, for instance. Or crashing out of his plane inverted, say, knocking himself out as he went through the canopy, that wasn't just a laugh.

The second tour of Vietnam. Seven hundred hours flying Chinooks in support of the First Cav. Phil was supposed to have been released from the Army, but there was such a shortage of chopper pilots—remember the 55 percent casualty rate from that first tour?—that he was sucked back into another tour. This time they stationed him fifteen miles from the DMZ, shuttling eighteen-year-old kids back and forth to battle. Well, mostly forth. The back part went to the dustoffs, medevac choppers that picked up the wounded and dead. The NVA used Phil's camp as a place to unload artillery; it was an easy lob across the DMZ. The shelling started at sunset and ended at sunrise. Phillip Knight from Gainesville, Florida, would try to get some sleep inside his tomb, a hole with three feet of sand on every side. *First round protection*, they called the tomb. You tried not to think about the second round. *Second round protection is getting your ass the hell out of the hole*, the guys joked. It was something, to go out and fly twelve hours, come home and try and sleep in that racket. They'd wake up in the morning never knowing how many choppers would be able to fly. Most were sprayed with shrapnel from the night's shelling. Phil Knight: Two tours. Purple Heart, Bronze Star, Soldiers Medal, Army Air Medal with twenty Oak Leaf clusters. So stop joking about the fucking knife on the parachute. The guy could wear an M-16 in flight. Other pilots would try to figure out how to get one in their cockpits too.

. . .

I mention the knife not because it looks so lethal or because it is a reminder of how dangerous our sport can be. It is a totem, sure, like a scar on your face. You look at it every morning. But after a while you don't need the reminder. The knife matters because it says something about the choices we make, about the kind of life we create from our minds, about the kind of intense and unforgiving attitude Phil tries to jam into the pilots he coaches. Some people live prepared for any eventuality, they are unsettled. They keep a bag packed, a knife at the ready. But there is a temptation in all of us to slowness, to settling down. Gravity and time do their inevitable work. "You have a choice my friend," Phil is telling me. Like Sergei he is a high priest of extreme flying. But where Sergei teaches skills and how to use them, Phil coaches your mind. His dogma is total commitment to every flight. He doesn't look away when he talks to me. If he blinks, I have not caught him at it. "You can either fly this all the way, and hard, or you can just have fun. There's nothing wrong with that. But there's only one way to fly it right."

The Oklahoma heat is eating at my back. Phil and I are standing on a big empty ramp at McCaw Field and you can hear nothing except wind in the weeds. The field stretches forever, a place where bombers used to stop on their Cold War practice runs. Now it is pure desolation. A small Tex-Mex restaurant serves greasy lunch to pilots passing through. The local car rental rents only trucks. McCaw has the virtue of being fifteen minutes flying time north of the Nationals site at Dennison. There are seven of us here, all coached by Phil. He is as impatient with our imperfections as he is good at repairing them. He is a man who has no place for drama. There is none of the playful acting you get with Sergei, the funny Soviet clown act he sometimes uses to get his students' attention. Phil doesn't have a teaching style that adjusts to his students, like Sergei does. A plane takes off, for instance. Five minutes into the sequence the canopy shatters in midair, turning the plane pretty much into a 200 mph convertible. The shaken pilot brings it to the ground and taxis back to the ramp. He is speechless for a full minute after shutting the engine down. No one can tell what happened. Did the canopy slap open during a snap roll? Did the pilot whack it from the inside with his helmet? Phil saw the whole thing. He is not interested in what happened or how the pilot is doing. He comes over to figure out how to repair the plane. That is all.

You can fly it all the way. I would like to. But in the moment when I come off the negative g's of a spin and into the hard pull of the hammerhead, I gray out. I am routinely flirting with black as I try to pull harder around corners. The longer the day goes on, the faster I go gray. In the mornings I can get around corners at seven g's without much of a problem. By afternoon, six puts me into a haze. An old instructor of mine once crashed this way, passing out as he tried to recover from a knife-edge spin on an April day when he hadn't had enough to eat or drink, when he hadn't slept well. As he felt the gray coming on, he'd pushed forward on the stick to unload the plane, accelerating his line toward the ground in the process. It was a choice between hitting the ground awake or asleep. The best way to stop g-grayouts is to stop the g's. He hauled back again on the stick just a moment before he pancaked in. Broke his back. Was scalped by the flying canopy. The NTSB called it a G-LOC accident, G-Induced Loss of Consciousness. Phil can see me backing off the g's as I fly, trying to stay awake. There are ways to deal with the gray, he tells me. We have a discussion about the vagaries of the human body, ways to trick our heart to do its work even when it is ten times its normal weight.

In flying no one wants to die in their sleep. Still, it happens every year. Some bright promise of American future in an F-18 pulls hard through the sky to hurry the plane around. Screaming along at five, six hundred miles an hour. One fast pop of the stick and it's off to sleep. Forever. "I had a bit of a faint up there, old man," the English pilots told their flight surgeons during World War I. Harry Head, an English neurologist with an oddly congruent name, interviewed dozens of WWI pilots and described many of the symptoms as we know them today: grayed-out vision ("a slight fog over the eyes"), sudden darkness, awakening with little memory of what happened. Head never managed to piece together a scientific explanation for the faints. Was it a lack of courage? Combat vapors? A neuralgic reaction to the noise of the plane?

"How did you go broke?" goes one memorable exchange with Hemingway from his Paris days. "Two ways," Papa says. "Slowly and then suddenly." So with G-LOC. In the first instance it settles on pilots like an ether. The brain holds a tiny emergency hoard of oxygenated blood that provides a cushion between g-loading and G-LOC. Inside that window, perhaps for as long as five seconds, it is possible to stay awake, even if you have lost your sight and hearing to the g's. The brain is running on reserve, shutting off your senses so it can concentrate on important things. Breathing. Heartbeats. If you prolong the g loads outside that window or load up before you've had time to regenerate that cushion, you'll snap out of consciousness. Instantly. Under a fast enough load, you can blink out without even the gray and quiet phase. Ten g's in less than a second and maintained for a couple of seconds can euthanize the best of us.

The Navy teaches pilots to drop their chins and say the word "hook" before straining their stomachs as the g's mount. The stomach straining—think of doing a situp—helps keep blood trapped in the upper body; the "k" in "hook" forces pilots to shut off the back of their throats, sealing up their chest pressure like knotting off a balloon. The technique adds about a g and a half of resistance. The Air Force teaches a similar system, though it asks pilots to keep their throats open so they can still communicate. Military flyers also have the benefit of anti-g suits that inflate like air bags whenever the plane loads up. The pressure keeps blood from pooling in their feet. Still, a Navy survey found 15 to 30 percent of pilots in operational squadrons had passed out at one time or another. Since one of the symptoms of G-LOC is amnesia—50 percent of subjects G-LOCed in centrifuges didn't remember it happening—that suggests that a third of military pilots have passed out in their multimillion-dollar cockpits. In some cases, the LOC can last two minutes. The good news, as it were, is that you die in your sleep.

"Hoooooook." I am grunting and grumbling through the bottom corners of my flight, fighting to keep my vision from graying away. "Good, stick it in there, stick it in, get on it," Phil is coming at me loud on the radio. "Okay and off." I pop the stick forward hard. I am seeing again. I pull the plane around on my back and dive straight down. 180. Pull. Eight g's. *Hoooooook.* I swivel my head left, all 160 pounds of it. I can see fine, out over the wing, to set my line. "Okay, get off." The straining is unnatural, but it works. Misused it can actually cause me to pass out, by pressing blood *away* from my head. A couple of times I flirt with just this mistake, grunting enthusiastically at the wrong moment and feeling as if someone has hit a switch in my eyes. But each time I remain awake at least long enough to unload the plane, shedding g's, as the world comes glistening back into place. I set the line. Then pull over the top. Down again. "Again," Phil says.

The body doesn't want to fly like this. No other activity creates quite the same problems. The positive g's accelerate our heartbeats and put pressure on our bodies. Neck pain is endemic with aerobatic pilots. At night now I can hear my spine crackling. Not cracking, *crackling.* And G-LOC is just one worry. As you take more and more negative g's, you are at greater risk for the wobblies, the secret code word of the sport, rarely discussed openly. The airline pilots in aerobatics know that the wobblies, a kind of instant-on vertigo, are a one-word ticket to retirement. "It's the most frightened I've ever been in a plane," an Unlimited pilot told me about his first taste of vertigo. "I've thought I was going to hit the ground five or six times in my career. But this was the only time I was really scared. I was flying along. I went level and suddenly I had no sense of balance or perspective. All I could do was sit there and try and hold the stick steady. I had time to just think. 'I'm going to hit the ground hard. And it's really going to hurt.' But it cleared up before I did. I landed." It took weeks before he felt normal; months before he could fly again. And the wobblies still return unpredictably, each time demanding as much as a month of recovery. They became for him, as they are for many Unlimited pilots, the wall past which he can train no more.

You learn tricks to avoid them. Don't stare at the sun. Don't turn from side to side while you fly. Don't whip your head around. Once, sitting in the cockpit of a Boeing as it leveled off at cruise, an Unlimited pilot I know propped his head back on the headrest for a few seconds. A stewardess came in to bring some drinks. She was laughing at something in the cabin behind them. He snatched his head around to see her, to get in on the joke and, instantly, it was as if the plane was pulling six g's straight up. He shot forward in his seat and grabbed the control yoke of the plane with both hands, preparing to jam the nose down furiously to stop the climb. Then he glanced at the electronic attitude indicator: everything was level. The stewardess was not careening screaming against the roof of the plane. Visually, all was well. Mentally it was a mess. The copilot looked warily over at the captain, who was now clutching the yoke with all his might, starting to sweat. Locked up like a sculpture: Desperation. No one uttered a word.

The wobblies come from a disorientation of the central nervous system. No one is certain what causes it. The best theory is that extensive exposure to negative g forces can dislocate small crystals on the ganglia inside the ear. These small hairs are surrounded by fluid. The movement of fluid across the hairs, together with our eyes and other senses, tells the body what's up and down. The fast negative g forces may displace some of the crystals that coat these hairs, in the way you might break ice on a lake with a stick. When the pilot pulls hard positive, the crystals are reset in a different pattern. The ganglia begin sending incorrect signals to the brain, signals that disagree with what the pilot sees outside. Chaos ensues. Wobblies are an awful dividend of the explosive pain of negative g's, that unmatchable, hateful cranial pressure. Negative g's are nothing like positive g's, a pain that can be managed or strained away. There is no maneuver to stop the negative g pressure, nothing to block the flow of blood to the head. It is like turning on a fire hose and pinching the end shut. There is no alternative to the pain except simply enduring.

It is maybe surprising that in a machine-driven sport our bodies become our ultimate point of reference. I certainly struggle to understand it at times. There is so much external data, so many sounds and sights and feelings pouring in, that I don't have the presence of mind to ignore them and just feel.

"Sit down," Sergei says to me one day as he tries to teach me to ignore what I am seeing around me. We are trying to correct my uplines, which are tilted about 5 degrees too much to the positive. Instead of climbing straight up, I am flying at about an 85 percent angle and staring out over the wing as I try to correct. I seesaw the plane back and forth, now too much, now too little. I settle down into a lawn chair next to Sergei's car. He leans over me and points his Revos at me. "Okay," he says. He grabs the chair and drops me over onto my back. I am looking up at the sky.

"What is telling you that you are on your back?"

"My eyes?" I offer.

"Your eyes, yes. But also your back. Your butt. And your inner ear. Just feel. Don't look."

My brain hasn't yet learned what straight up feels like. So though my eyes tell me I am on a vertical line, my back is telling me something else as I sit in the cockpit. I am mis-learning, teaching my brain the wrong feelings.

Phil spots the problem immediately. It is the kind of fix he is best at, tweaking the shape of a figure in the sky. Sergei tends to worry about the overall flow of a sequence. Phil worries about the parts, the sharp little details that mark a figure that scores well. My lines are not helped any by the grayouts. "Strain," he shouts on the radio. He sends me back up in the sky again and again to fly straight up and down lines. Twenty minutes at a time. He shouts up minor adjustments on the radio. "Positive," he'll radio, letting me know I am still short of 90 degrees. "Negative," he'll say when I go over on my back, overcompensating. Somewhere around my thirtieth line

I begin to get it correct. The lines start to unspool perfectly in the sky. I can fly them without a glance outside. Two days before Nationals, I am finally feeling free in the plane, comfortable with the speed and the possibility of surprise. I have made the choice to do this all the way. "Good," Phil says on the radio. "Now, harder."

There is a species of thriller in which

a man discovers himself . . .

There is a species of thriller in which a man discovers himself suddenly in the middle of abstract and complex difficulties. The high-brow version of this character might be Kafka's Gregor Samsa, who awakes to discover that he is a bug. But there are other forms. "Perhaps you were at the theater tonight as you say," the policeman observes as a wet Paris night empties itself onto our pulp-novel hero. "But then how do you explain the gunpowder on your sleeves, monsieur?" The hero is genuinely perplexed. He *was* at the theater. He is certain he was not involved in a murder. Yet the gunpowder is unquestionably there. A case against him is laid brick by brick. Yes, he does have bullets in his pocket. Where *did* they come from? Sure he speaks Bulgarian—he picked it up in college— but he is not a spy. The bricks of his life are rearranged into a new and strange edifice. It looks like a jail cell. It is as if you left your house one morning and returned at night to find a new building in its place. Perhaps you drive around the block a few times. You wonder if you are lost. You park your car and walk up to the house. You recognize the color of the bricks, the tone of the lamps, the ironwork that once girded the back porch now winding up around a mailbox. These are the bricks of your own life. They have been moved. You do not like the result at all. But you no more know how to reverse the process than you know how it started. It is not simply that the familiar has become mysterious. The familiar has become a foreign country. The language here is guttural, the water is bitter, no one smiles. But, perhaps you begin to realize: this is where I am supposed to live.

This is my country now, I am an immigrant in my own life. It is late at night and I am standing in front of a mirror in a walkup hotel outside Dennison, Texas. The night is hot and sticky, it coats my cold windows with dew as it fights the air-conditioning. I am naked and dripping with water from a late shower. And I am unrecognizable. My hips are marked with garish blue welts the size of a palm print, bruises from the pressure of my seat harness. My stomach ripples in the fluorescent light; my tired body freed of a dozen extra pounds from sweat that comes faster than I can drink. I rock my head from side to side, hearing the cracks where my spine is tight from incessant g loading. I close my eyes and begin mind-flying my sequence: dive in, hard pull, push to horizontal. The engine screams in my head. I twist around on the cheap carpet, dancing through my routine as if I were in the air, hard lefts and rights. After twenty minutes I stop to dry my hair. I lie down. I begin flying again.

There is a psychological subtext to these tales: we are all guilty. Here is what I mean. Kafka gets interesting only when Samsa begins accepting that he is a bug. Our pulp hero emerges as a man only when he begins to wonder if perhaps he is a murderer. Maybe something does lurk inside him that he didn't know was there. Maybe there is something good too. Sometimes our lives become mysteries to us.

. . .

Thunder crackles outside. I am trying, but failing, to sleep. Monday morning, three A.M., Dennison, Texas. This is Nationals week. It is my first trip and I am rattling inelegantly with nerves. A perfect flight will demand that I take what I have done so far and use it at last as a base for real flying, for a stab at perfection. This is a graduation for me, with all its attendant pressures. The training has pounded technique into my flying. Now I have one shot to turn the preparation into something like art, to try to fly what is in my head. And I am not honestly sure I can do it. What I am learning in the air, over and over again, is humility and a worrying certainty that nothing we fly in the sky can match what we dream of in our heads. Our hopes outrun our lives. My faith that I can do anything is being tested by the demand of actually achieving it. It is one thing to sit and dream of great flying; quite another to manage it. It is one thing to sit and dream of a great life; quite another to live it. This seems like something a child could figure out. It is disconcerting to be learning it now.

Around Dennison we are probably all awake. For Unlimited pilots like David Martin or Kirby Chambliss or Alan Bush, the stakes are high. A year's training and a lifetime's plans and hopes concatenated into a week's worth of judgments. Maybe they are asleep. There is no point in being awake.

I turn over and listen to the rain.

The clear, hot days that tormented my training flights a week ago, the turbulent afternoon air that lingered over the Southwest, are gone. On those long Oklahoma afternoons I struggled not only with the aerobatics but also with unstable air that bounced the plane every time I tried to stay level. Now, coming up from the Gulf of Mexico, a thick, wet layer of air promises to avenge the parched weeks just passed. Days of these thunder waves are forecast. No National Championship has ever been canceled because of weather, but in at least one year, the championship has been decided by a single flight instead of the usual three.

Monday goes to rain. Tuesday too. Wednesday is a blur of impatient futility, trips to Wal-Mart, long lunches. We sit at the airport and talk until we run out of things to say. And every passing day we are all losing our touch for our planes. Some pilots here have flown four flights a day every day for a month. They are nearly ticking with spring-loaded energy. Now they must sit as their skills erode, as their touch is anesthetized by the passage of time. On Thursday, finally, a break: the morning clouds clear faster than usual and we are suddenly flying. But the clear comes at a price: the clouds have been pushed off by a relentless northerly wind that is now howling through the box at nearly fifty miles an hour. It makes flying like trying to cross an iced-over lake on skates in the wind. Simply by turning my plane from north to south I'll incur a hundred-miles-an-hour speed penalty as the tailwind turns into a headwind. Lines flown into the strong wind will seem to creak by; downwind lines will go three or four times faster than I'm used to. The natural bee-bop rhythm of my sequence, a dance I've painstakingly memorized in the last month, is going to become a stuttering waltz.

The Unlimited power pilots like David and Kirby and

Alan are the first into the box. Kirby shoots into the opening maneuver of his sequence—a series of powerful snap rolls shot off as he flies straight down—and pulls out hard into the headwind, drawing a nearly perfect figure despite the gale. You can see his plane hurrying a bit on the downwind, rushing as the wind pushes it from behind, but his sense of speed is so acute that the forty-knot difference is immediately apparent to him and almost irrelevant. He moves through the sky with a syncopated pace, like a concert pianist playing against an orchestra that is alternately drunk and on speed. Slamming and staggering his way through the flight, he finishes first. Close behind him is David Martin, with a nearly perfect performance of his own. Alan Bush flies his tiny Velox, a one-of-a-kind aerobatic prototype, into seventh place.

I am flying tenth in the Sportsman order. A good slot, far enough down so I can watch some of my competitors working against the wind. There are some spectacular failures: a pilot who flies nearly every figure out of the box, for instance. You can see palpable panic and confusion in his flight as the wind pounds him closer to disqualification. He flirts with the "dead-line" on the east side of the field. Crossing it means instant disqualification for flying too close to the crowd. At the last moment he tucks back inside the box. He lands long, fighting the plane all the way down.

I am sitting quietly in an air-conditioned car just off the main ramp watching this. My breathing is even. I close my eyes at intervals and imagine parts of my sequence. Four days of sitting around have left me feeling less sharp, like years without speaking a language. I think I can express myself clearly in the air. I hope so. I haven't had a chance to fly the Dennison box yet. This is more important than it may seem. The box is clearly marked and should be easy to pick out from the sky, but there are local peculiarities you can learn only in the air. I've tried to pick up hints from my friends. *Watch the water tower. Pass it and you are out.* But there is no substitute for seeing it myself. I can feel the rust in my instincts. But my last flight left a wonderful taste. I took off and worked my way out over the nearby lakes and practiced vertical lines. Below me, the last week of a Texas summer was unwinding on the backs of jet-skis and power boats, all tracing white lines on the water. I came in low over the lake, fast, and pulled at 1,000 feet for the ride up to 4,000, straight up. I kicked over on a wing, and then shot straight down to 2,000, a full power dive, before pulling out again. On that downline I put the plane through clean 360-degree rolls, just to get the feel of the air moving on the wings. Everything felt solid. More important, it felt fast and hard. I was flying the plane fiercely now, routinely starting off from speeds well into the plane's red-line zone. There was no ballet in my flying.

As the Unlimited pilots finish their sequences, Phil Knight, the "air boss" in charge of keeping planes coming and going, holds a mandatory pilot briefing under the broad white tent on the east side of the field. Everyone wears his nerves: quick glances around the tent, laughter too loud, a heavy silence when Phil asks for questions. He turns to a giant blown-up aerial photo of the land around the airport and begins pointing out key landmarks. As our turns come up we'll be cleared to depart by the starter on the ramp, he explains. At that point we'll taxi to the active runway, take off, and head to a holding area at

2,000 feet to the southwest of the box. There we'll orbit in a large oval pattern, keeping an eye on the traffic in the box, until we're cleared into the second holding area, at 3,500 feet on the northwest corner of the box. There we can orbit, roll inverted to check our belts, and wait. Once we're cleared into the box there will be no radio chatter. Pilots are to stay off frequency while another pilot is working. No one wants the distraction of another voice in his ear while he pulls through a sequence. There is an additional complexity, Phil warns us: our powered aerobatic flights will be intermixed with the U.S. National Glider Aerobatic competition. The gliders are towed into the box area by a small Cessna. The Cessna is underpowered. It will be fighting the wind. The gliders, of course, have no engines. The wind is so strong they have considered canceling their flight, worried they will be blown too far from the field, forced to land on some suburban playground. But they will fly. It means more traffic for us.

I wander back into some air-conditioning and make a few small notes on my sequence card—"Pull harder here" or "float longer"—to adjust for the wind. I won't have time to look at the card in flight so I try to memorize the adjustments. Ultimately, I'll have to manage it all by feel. As the sixth and seventh pilots in the sequence are strapping in, I head out to the plane. I give the Extra a quick preflight, checking over things I've already checked and rechecked. I am flying with about twenty minutes of fuel, betting I'll spend less than five minutes in each of the holds. I pull my parachute out and slip into it, tightening the harness around my legs and chest. Cliff, the starter, comes over to check that everything looks okay.

"Gas?" He is a small, meticulous man, the sort you would trust with your insurance policy, or the spare keys to your house. I hit the master switch, which brings the gas and engine gauges on line. He looks it over. Carefully. Looks me in the eyes for a moment. Then his clipboard. "Okay," he says. "Strap in." I climb in and fasten my belts, grinding them down hard. Cliff looks in again to make sure everything is wired in right. Nervous pilots have taken off with lap belts undone, a problem that emerges only when they roll upside down for a belt check. I'm fine, I thought. I'm fine. "Fire up," he says. "Good luck."

I run through the prestart checklist. I've memorized it by now but consult it on paper just in case. In the cockpit I start the ritual I've done hundreds of times since learning to fly. I shout "clear prop" and hit the starter with my left hand, holding the stick back against the wind with my right. The engine kicks over and I feed in fuel with the mixture lever. I settle the engine down to about 1,000 rpms and put on my headset, fastening down the chin strap. I taxi out, rolling my neck to stay loose. The airport around me is eerily quiet. To my right, a cluster of six judges sits under individual white sun umbrellas, each with a recorder on one side and a spotter on the other. The spotters will call out the figures just before they are flown; the recorder will jot down the zero to ten score. All the results will go into a computer program that factors out any possible judging bias. They stare up at a plane above me with perfectly tranquil expressions. They look as if they could be at a cricket match.

I am sweating in the heat, and the light breeze through my storm window does nothing to cool the summer air. I taxi down to runway 18. I'll be departing straight south, dead into the wind. The wind sock is fully extended, meaning that there is a thirty-knot wind on the ground. It appears to be mostly from the south with a little bit of east component. At altitude I'll check it again. It's not uncommon to find different winds in the air than on the ground, so flying based on the wind sock is a recipe for error. I close my eyes for a moment, looking for nerves. No sign of them yet. The engine runup is clean. It is time to fly the perfect flight, I say to myself. I taxi into the center of the broad runway, push the throttle forward, and lift off into a sharp 45-degree climb. I turn right at about 500 feet and head out to the first holding area. I am trying to make everything I do precise: every turn stops hard, I level off with a clean pop on the elevator, I make my holding-pattern orbits in a nice one-turn-two rhythm.

After a couple of these orbits in pattern one I am cleared to pattern two. I arrive at the second pattern and climb to 4,000 feet, 500 feet above the top of the box. The extra altitude will allow me to pick up another ten knots before I start the sequence. I fly in gentle circles, watching as the south wind pushes me northward over the ground. The wind is stronger than I have seen in competition before, but I think I can manage it. I line up over a north-south road and look carefully to see if I am being pushed from side to side. Nothing. The wind is pure south. All good news, easier to keep aligned.

The glider pilot ahead of me is fighting to get into the right position. I begin to worry about gas. *Why did you take off with only twenty minutes of gas?* I thought I'd be in and out of the box in ten minutes tops. I reach down and adjust the fuel flow through the engine.

The moment I release the knob my concentration shatters. It is like breaking a pane of glass. I feel nerves leaking into my hands and my feet. *Shit. Come on.* The glider pilot is finally clear of the box. "The box is yours," Phil tells me. I turn inbound. I have drifted about a mile too far north, now I must fight back into position through that headwind while the judges wait on the ground. "Where are you?" Phil asks a moment later. "Inbound," I say tersely. I am right at 4,000 feet and the bottoms of the clouds are so close that I am dipping in and out of mist. I'll be diving in from here for as much speed as possible. But the low ceiling means that if I pull up too high, I could shoot into a cloud. I add the ceiling to my list of worries. I ease toward the north edge of the box, adjusting for the wind. A quick glance at my altimeter shows that I am 300 feet lower than I would like. The judges are waiting for me. It feels all wrong. I dive in anyhow.

The nose goes over hard in a 45-degree downline. The airspeed starts to climb and wind shakes the canopy. I am diving as fast as I can, with full power to the engine, which is as noisy as I have ever heard it. At 3,000 feet I wag my wings for the judges, the sign that I am starting my sequence. But I have begun too far north, fooled by a rookie mistake, the parallaxed view from my cockpit. The optical illusion makes it look as if I am closer to the box than I am. When I eagerly pull level and get ready to start my sequence I am still well outside. I sit, pissing airspeed for thirty lethal seconds. I look off to the left and pick out a hangar that is coming up abeam, a landmark I selected earlier as a start-point for my sequence. Since I cannot see the box directly below my plane, it's the best clue I have as to my position. As the hangar passes my wing I pull hard to vertical for my first figure. The upline is good. I pivot my head to the left wing and am suddenly nervous. I snap out of it in less than a second—*Fly the plane*—but the moment was enough. I've pushed my line off of vertical and I don't have the time or speed to get it back. Not a fatal error, but one that will make a good score difficult. I ease back over to horizontal flight, pull back the power and kick the plane into a spin, the next figure in my sequence. It's a nice, clean entry and my recovery line is dead vertical at the ground. Maybe I'm okay, I think. I slam the plane level. Count an extra beat for the head-wind and pull up again. Up I go until the plane runs out of air-speed. I feed in left rudder, a touch of right stick, and pivot on my wing. A hammerhead turn. I set my downline, pull, and check my altimeter as I come out to level flight. I am low by the 300 feet I blew at the start of my sequence. As I pull up into my next figure, an Immelman turn, I exaggerate the top of the figure, an arcing upward loop, to squeeze out an extra hundred feet of altitude. I roll upright. Check the altimeter: 2,100 feet. The 300 feet are still missing. That leaves me 600 for the next figure, a half-loop down. I have done the half-loop in less, but only by pulling eight g's. I still have two more altitude-losing figures in the sequence. I do the math as I set up. I could possibly manage it in 500 feet, but then I would need equally hard pulls on the later figures and there is *still* a chance I would be out low and zero the whole flight. What I am about to start is like the final, energetic tumbling run in a gymnastics exhibition. Once I'm under way it will be difficult to break it off elegantly. And repetitive eight-g turns are a high-risk proposition for me. I exhale. It's a no-choice. I wing wag to signify a break in my sequence and pull up and out of the box. The break will be a deduction, but a small penalty compared to what I would get for blowing the low-lines on the box. That mistake gets the death penalty from judges: a zero for the entire flight and a guarantee of last place.

I hurry up to 3,000 feet and reposition myself, well away from the windward side of the box. I dive down and pick up my sequence at 2,500 feet. I roll inverted and manage the half-loop at a comfortable six g's. I barrel through the rest of the sequence. It is a sloppy flight, nothing like the air sculpture I was making in Oklahoma during my best training flights. I land furious. I sit in the cockpit nauseated. It is not the heat or g's. There is no one to blame for the flight but me. It has been a miserable performance, filled with a child's errors. With the weather closing in, this may have been it. One flight for the championship.

I park the plane and wander into the pilots' lounge to get my computerized scores. They are the sevens and eights of an amateur, with few nines. No tens. And one even worse mistake: coming back from my altitude break I forgot to perform a 90-degree competition turn that was part of my sequence. Just left it out. Zero, on a positioning maneuver that should have been a certain 10 for me. Thirteenth place. "What the hell happened up there?" Alan asks me later. I should have had a top-ten finish. I am too upset to answer. Back in our first flights Alan used to say he admired my anger. That intensity had allowed him to take me from no solo time in the plane to my first competition in two weeks. But now it is getting in the way. I am so pissed that I cannot fly straight.

The last few planes are coming back into the hangar. Alan takes me aside. He has the relaxed mien of a man who has seen everything in the air. "Look," he says, "you have to just let yourself fly the plane. You have to trust what you know. Stop thinking up there. You left a figure out? You had to make that mistake some day. Okay, you've made it now. But this was your third competition flight so have some fucking perspective. Let's go have some beer and we can sit around and hope that you'll get to fly again. You won't make the same mistakes."

"Okay," I struggle out.

He smiles. "You'll make a whole new set of 'em."

Friday morning is solidly overcast, pushing any chance of a flight until deep in the afternoon. Just as well, since I spent most of the night with my best friend in Dallas, drowning my sorrows in the g-strings of University of Texas cheerleaders moonlighting at a local strip club. One of them wanted to have a long conversation with me about becoming a doctor. I didn't have any advice. I head out to my ritual breakfast at the IHOP: pancakes with a crowd of pilots and truck drivers. I am less angry than yesterday.

The clouds start to clear. The fog that has been wrapping up the minimalls and gas stations burns away as the day passes. The horizon emerges to the east. Then to the south we can see the outlines of Dallas. And in the early afternoon the sky clears over the field itself, giving all of us who want to fly better a final chance at redemption. I am late in the draw and will probably not take to the air until around five. The south wind is stronger than yesterday, but I am better prepared for it. My first flight has at least left me with a nothing-to-lose attitude for this second attempt. I feel loose as I strap in, take off, and hit holds one and two. There is no delay and I smash into the box hard and fast, just like I want. In my fourth competition flight ever I feel at home and as comfortable as if I were fishing on a spring day on the Rio Grande. The screaming propeller is like river music. I pull up hard and smooth to my first figure—eight-and-a-half g's without a hint of grayout. The whole sequence is tight and smooth. The sky is growing pink as I finish, electric with a good effort. The flight improves my position to eleventh overall, one spot short of my goal of top ten. It is an unusually close year. The difference between the first and second place competitor was 1/100th of a point; between my eleventh and first are less than five percentage points off the lead, 79.4 percent to 83 percent. The missed figure in my first flight is the difference between eleventh and tenth. But the second flight was what I was really trying for. It was a flight that was even better than what I had in my head. It was the work of a transformed man, a remade pilot. There is also good news for the pilots I admire. Nine years after his first Nationals, David Martin has won the overall Unlimited championship, a good start for a run at Leo's record. Kirby Chambliss is second. And he is leaving in a hurry. Bound for that bridge in China.

Once I met a man
who had put his hand
through a table.

Once I met a man who had put his hand through a table. It had already been a strange night. I was in Calcutta. I had landed shortly after midnight on a flight from Bangkok and the city was blacked out. *An electrical error,* they explained at the airport. In town, Mother Teresa was dying. I tried to find my way to her home for the sick and dying in the dark. Outside my taxicab all of Calcutta pressed at me through the black night. It began to rain lightly. The water cut the dust in the air. The sweat began to dry on my face, caking the dirt there. The city was unnavigable. I found a hotel where I could wait for morning.

In the lobby there was a small old man sitting by candlelight, since there was no electricity. My body was on another time zone so we sat up talking as the city outside quieted itself, relaxed by the rain maybe, and sought some peace in sleep. The lobby was an Indian attempt to do something magnificent. It looked like an American Howard Johnson's that hadn't been refurbished since the Eisenhower years. The furniture was all long and brown and uncomfortable. The glass doors were cracked in a few places. The sun films on the windows had gone purple with age. The elevator wasn't working—*an electrical error*—so guests were making their way up and down the stairs. An ice machine stood against one wall in the lobby, as out of place as if someone had put a urinal there. The ice was melting, but the guests came down all night to take what was left in any plastic container they could find.

The man was from the hill country, a long way from here. He described it in vivid terms. The taste of the water, the way the women laughed, how he had run on the streets there as a boy. When he was in his early teens, his father had sent him up into the hills to work at one of the tea plantations. It was hard work, but he didn't know any better and was happy to be free from his house. He liked the company of the other men. They were older than he, but they sang together as they worked and he felt a part of something important, even if it was just the harvest of the tea. They worked every day, clearing the land in the spring, harvesting the tea in the fall. At night they returned to their small shacks. Dinner was prepared by some lower-caste women. Steamed vegetables and cold rice. Tea, of course, too.

In the camp was a quiet older man. He was treated with great respect. He had reached that point in the Hindu life cycle where a man begins to renounce his belongings. There is no explicit age for this. When the man feels he is finally ready to renounce the things of this world, he begins to shed them. Perhaps he first abandons something easy. Spicy foods, say. Maybe he is forty. A few years later he embraces the *bramacharya*, and leaves behind intimacy with his wife. He gives away his belongings. He dresses simply. He stops earning money and begins asking it from strangers. And with everything he leaves behind, he moves closer to an imagined purity, to nirvana, to a state of complete cleanliness. It is the most beautiful thing on earth. This was how Gandhi described watching his uncle die and complete the last stages of the detachment. The old man, in his last moments, clawing at his wrist to throw off his final possession, a gold bracelet. He wanted to go into the next world completely unencumbered. He wished to leave everything behind.

In the tea camp this old man had very nearly reached this state of beautiful enlightenment. Some days he would come out to the plantation and work with the much younger men, but he was feeble and ate so little that he had to stop at regular intervals to take on some food and a little water. He was like a train, the young men joked. *Choo-choo*, they called him, but respectfully, the way you might address a small joke to your father from time to time. Other days he would just come out and watch the men harvest. He seemed to get a special pleasure from watching the way they worked, how they were hypnotized by the movement of their own knives, transported so that they were outside their bodies almost. The knives moving quickly along the rows, but no danger to anyone, no more threatening than a man blinking or smiling. The old man seemed to feel at one with the men, and celebrated both the good days of growing and the bad days when the rains might damage something it had taken a long time to build.

For no particular reason, he slept on the same part of the floor as the man I met in the hotel that night in Calcutta. Perhaps it was because one was old and the other was young. I don't know and my interlocutor at the hotel never mentioned the details. But at night before they would go to sleep, the old man would tell the young one about how his mind had been growing clearer with age, how simple the world now appeared. As he gave things up, he explained, the world started to look different. Instead of seeing people, he could see their souls. Instead of seeing trees, he would hear the leaves speaking to him. Solid objects became like clouds to him. He could walk through walls if he wanted. He could pour boiling water through his arm, the way you might run it through a pile of tea leaves as you prepared breakfast. He could put his hand through solid wood. The man I met that night in Calcutta said he didn't really believe any of this at the time. He was young. He had many years of spicy food and sex and money ahead of him. And he was so respectful of his elders that it never occurred to him to ask the old man to prove he could do these things. They were just ramblings, he suspected.

But the story stayed with him. He aged himself. And in the Hindu tradition, he began giving things up. About a year or so before I met him he had given up his family in the hills and wandered down to Calcutta to be nearer to the Ganges. He lived off alms. And as soon as he came to the city, he told me, he too began seeing the world in pieces, not as a whole. People would talk to him and he would be unable to hear what they were saying, so absorbed was he by the colors they radiated. Once someone from his home village recognized him on the street and came up to greet him. But he was so overwhelmed by the music that traveled with this old friend that he didn't realize who he was until several days later, when he recognized the music as a song they had once sung together as children. Recently, he told me, he had begun to see vibrations in the world. He thought he saw buildings moving. He worried about holding on to things. One day he was sitting quietly on a street, holding a little bowl and waiting for money. He was sitting next to a fruit stall. The fruit stall was vibrating. He looked at it carefully. It was like looking at steam or clouds. So he stood up and walked over to the table in front of the stall, a table piled high with ripening mangoes. He looked around to see if anyone was watching. Really, this was absurd, he thought. This was going to be the final test of his sanity. Perhaps it was that he was not eating as much as he should. Maybe he was losing his mind. He looked around again. The proprietor of the stall was off doing something else. The old man took his left hand and pushed the sleeve of his white robe up along his right arm. Then he placed his right arm over the table. It felt hot, the way steam does. And then he pushed his hand into the table and out the other side.

In 1981 Sergei Boriak was flying at a competition in Tula. It was a shitty day. The clouds made a low ceiling on what was one of the ugliest parts of the Soviet empire. From the air you couldn't tell the difference between earth and sky. To fly aero-

batics in such a dimensionless world was disorienting and
dangerous. You were lucky to get through your sequence at
all. You were happy to get back on the ground.

Boriak had just joined the team and one of his mentors, if
you could call him that, was Jurgis Kayris, from Lithuania.
Jurgis couldn't really mentor anyone. It was like trying to
learn from the sea. Karyis was the most passionate man Sergei
had ever met and he admired the passion. When Jurgis was
angry, the whole world was angry. When he was sad, it was as
if every mother in Lithuania wept with him. He had a sense of
humor that was like an automatic door: it kept opening and
closing every time you got near it. He was a man who was all
emotion. He couldn't control them any more than the sun can
control its heat. Eventually this was how Boriak would come
to beat him, by recognizing that Jurgis's emotions were his
weakness. They made him inconsistent. At times, though,
they made him brilliant. Boriak was a young kid, but watching
Kayris fly in those days made him feel old. "It was like watching someone break in a horse," he said. "You can't tell if they
are young or old, just if they know what they are doing." Jurgis made Sergei feel old and tired and like he didn't know
what he was doing.

You had to fly. Despite the bad weather, this was an
important contest. When Jurgis took off, his plane disappeared behind clouds as he made his way up into the box.
The wind picked up and it was cold. Sergei watched carefully
from the ground, like an old man watching young men playing at a game he had once loved. Kayris came in low, but fast
somehow. Who knew where he got the speed? He came into

the box furiously, like he was angry. *When Jurgis was angry, the whole world was angry.* The fury created something perfect. Sergei had never seen anything like it. In the coming decades he would see something close maybe a half-dozen times. The absolutely perfect flight. Such a thing was supposed to not exist. It was something you tried for, but, of course, you never achieved it. The whole point, striving and striving, was never getting to the place until the very end, if at all. But there was Jurgis. Ideal. His version of paradise looked like this: the visibility of a blizzard, the tranquility of a hurricane. It was as if he was flying and watching himself from the outside. "This is the ultimate form of flying," Sergei said. It was like the artist Willem De Kooning, speaking of some of his most astonishing work, pictures of naked women that might have been God's designs for Eve. "I am the source of a rumor concerning these drawings, and it is true that I made them with closed eyes." Beauty in the world, true, perfect beauty in this world, requires a detachment from it.

This turns out to be, in a way, the philosophy behind tumbling your airplane in the sky. There had to be a philosophy. You didn't need one to roll or loop the plane, even to spin it. That was simple flying. Physics was as good a philosophy as you could have, as good a one as you needed. It explained everything, how the pull on the stick put the nose up and over. But to tumble the plane, to detach the plane from the air and let it snap out of control in the sky, you needed to believe in something. In tumbling the plane you are making it stop flying altogether, every surface. You are far outside of physics. The best pilots in the world cannot regularly predict where their tumbles will end. Engineers can't explain what is happening in any detail. There are too many variables. Tumbling is at once the most violent thing you could do in an airplane and the most wonderful. But it requires faith. More people have stood on the top of Everest than have mastered the art of tumbling an airplane with precision and grace. It isn't a task to be taken lightly.

Getting the plane to tumble is difficult. The challenge sat in front of me like a complex math problem. Without a firm grounding in algebra, geometry, and calculus it was impossible to attempt. The idea was to stop the lift on every surface of the airplane all at once through a series of control inputs. Then, with lift destroyed, to use the propeller to flip the airplane around in the sky. It is possible to think of every airplane as having a hinge point, somewhere near its center of gravity. The best planes for tumbling are like a quarter, where the center of gravity and the center of mass are one and the same. In such planes it is possible to tumble with the speed and beauty of a flipped coin. But even so, you have to keep the plane from flying again the whole time. As it flips in the sky the plane will ceaselessly try to reattach the airflow to its wings. Almost as soon as the nose is pointing down the plane will try to start flying again. It is like trying to balance on a ledge. When you begin to feel yourself tipping you must make an immediate adjustment. It is best to try to start your tumble on a line going up, when the plane has the most upward inertia. This is a way to keep the nose from dropping too quickly, to keep the wings from flying again.

You can start the maneuver in any number of ways, from a snap or a regular roll, from a 45-degree line up or down. But once you are going around you cannot let the plane start flying again. This is the most difficult part of the tumble. When the plane flies you have an attachment to something, you can feel connected to the plane and to the air. But, Sergei warns, "when you are tumbling you feel nothing." The plane is at zero g almost the whole time. When you are pulling high g's or pushing negative g's you are being jerked in or out of your seat. With zero g you feel nothing at all while the world is tumbling around you violently. You aren't attached to anything but the controls. If you are lucky and flying well, the plane actually starts to accelerate. You tumble ever faster. It frightens you even more, frankly. These are maneuvers that are not allowed in regular competition. They are simply too hard to score, impossible even for the best pilots to manage with any consistency.

Then you must recover. You never know how the tumble is going to end. So you also need to have the skill and confidence to recover from anything. Will you be in a spin? Will you end up diving straight down? Perhaps your nose will be pointed up, zero air speed, waiting for a tailslide to whip you around. It is the ultimate test of flying, and it is not flying at all. It is like De Kooning's ultimate test of seeing, done with his eyes closed. Or Kayris's ultimate test of flying, done with no reference to the ground. To master the ability to not fly at all you must be able to fly wonderfully. Only when you have total faith in your connection with the air can you release it.

I start with inverted spins. It takes months to get to the point where I can tumble, but the inverted spins are a good start. They are dangerous in their small way. The optics can fool you. It is not always easy to tell that you are spinning upside down. If you put in the controls to stop what you think is an upright spin you will accelerate your inverted spin, making it harder to recover. If you are too enthusiastic about your inverted recovery you can press the plane into a crossover spin, in which it snaps from an inverted spin to an upright one, complicating recovery even more. I start with the upside down spins and repeat them until I am comfortable. Then flat spins, snap rolls. I develop a whole vocabulary of violent flight. One day I am ready to try a tumble. A late spring day. I am ready at last to graduate to the world of uncontrollability. I am ready to see, I hope, what I have been looking for in the air all along.

I once had a love affair that dragged on for years. Far too long, really, to the point where it was like a symphony that goes on a movement beyond what is really necessary. You sit in your seat and fidget. The composer is making the same points again, only louder. There is no innovation. It is not like Beethoven's Ninth, ending more spectacularly than it began. No, it is a forced march. Over and over again, she broke my heart. The phone rang: she was married. It rang again: she was pregnant. It rang: she missed me, could I come back. It rang: she was pregnant again. And I absolutely could not stop loving this woman. It was simply beyond my control. Every heartbreak was fresh. I was not the kind of man to whom this happened, but there it was. The phone rang. Could I come to see her?

What happens, I think, is that we begin to believe that if we just look at things long enough they will change. If we look at the fruit stall table with enough patience, with enough faith, it will become a cloud. One day we will walk right up to it and put our hands through the wood. It is that easy. All that is required is faith. Faith that we are good enough, that we deserve to have the world dissolve like this in front of us. Reordered as a sign of our piety. We have to trust that we have something innately pure and good in ourselves, that our original sin is simply the act of not believing this. From any position our lives are recoverable. And once we believe this we are really, finally free to live. This was what I was trying to learn in the air.

Why do I fly? For a while I thought it might be about trying to prove something to myself. Then I thought maybe it was chemical, the thrill-seeking. And even for a moment or more I thought it was about that love affair, as if there was something in the man I would be in the sky that would make us whole again. But I've concluded that it is about faith. Faith in the ability to see the world a certain way in your head and then live life so that it is so. Faith that everything is ultimately recoverable. Faith that something good waits for us after that night when we slow down on the motorcycle and the van comes from behind. So, more than any competition, the tumble is the final rite. To take to the skies and try it alone, not knowing where it will end, believing I can get from there to the ground safely. It is an act of pure faith. But to succeed I have to be willing to be out of control. What else is the purpose of living?

It is the kind of night to write poems about. Just twilight, soft and pink on the green Florida land below me. I take the plane high in the cool air. Eight thousand feet. It is very high. I am a novitiate in this kind of flight. I circle for a while, my mind patiently ironing out the fear. The sun races down. I take a breath. I have a vision in my head of what this should look like. I know how it should feel, how the violence will come like a punch and go away like a giggle. It should be wonderful and terrible at the same moment. To wit: You know from experience that this woman whom you love will damage you. You cannot resist her. It is too beautiful. It is all life and you can see it in the air between the two of you. You look into her eyes and they dissolve into a cloud. Her chest opens and you can put your hand inside. You are finally good enough and pure. I come back hard and fast on the stick. The plane whips up and I push it to the side, before it can spill off energy. The sky is pink outside. The sun is racing down. I hang on my wing. Then forward, everything forward, stick and rudders all at once and the plane is gone into a beautiful and terrifying chaos. I don't even try to control it. I just let it happen.

Paris
April 2002

ACKNOWLEDGMENTS

The author would like to acknowledge the help of Dorothy Cochrane of the National Air and Space Museum, and Budd Davisson and Annette Carson for their work on the history of aerobatics. He also wishes to thank Jeffery Jacobs and Professor Ezra Suleiman for providing extraordinary writing locations alongside the Pecos River in New Mexico and the Seine in Paris.

ABOUT THE AUTHOR

JOSHUA COOPER RAMO was raised in Los Ranchos, New Mexico, alongside the Rio Grande River. He began flying in his late teens and holds two U.S. national point-to-point airspeed records. He is currently training for a paraglider descent of New Mexico's highest peak. He joined *Time* in 1996 as the youngest senior editor in the magazine's history and went on to become its foreign editor and assistant managing editor. He is a member of the Council on Foreign Relations and the World Economic Forum's Global Leaders of Tomorrow, and is a Crown Fellow of the Aspen Institute and a cofounder of the U.S.-China Young Leaders Forum.